Your Simple Guide to a
HOME·BASED BUSINESS

Emilie Barnes & Sheri Torelli

D1371900

HARVEST HOUSE PUBLISHERS
Eugene, Oregon 97402

Unless otherwise marked, Scripture quotations are taken from the New American Standard Bible, © 1960, 1962, 1963, 1968, 1971, 1972, 1973, 1975, 1977, 1995 by The Lockman Foundation. Used by permission.

Cover by Terry Dugan Design, Minneapolis, Minnesota

If you would like more information on scheduling seminars and workshops, please contact:

Emilie Barnes
More Hours in My Day
2838 Rumsey Drive
Riverside, California 92506
(909) 682-4714
www.emiliebarnes.com

OR

Sheri Torelli
Accu-Pro Typing Service
2150 Whitestone Drive
Riverside, California 92506
(909) 787-9762
email: accupro@ez-access.com

YOUR SIMPLE GUIDE TO A HOME-BASED BUSINESS

Copyright © 1999 by Emilie Barnes and Sheri Torelli
Published by Harvest House Publishers
Eugene, Oregon 97402

Library of Congress Cataloging-in-Publication Data
  Barnes, Emilie.
    Your simple guide to a home-based business / Emilie Barnes and Sheri Torelli.
        p. cm.
      Includes bibliographical references.
    ISBN 0-7369-0057-8
    1. Home-based businesses—Management. 2. New business enterprise—management.
    I. Torelli, Sheri, 1956– . II. Title.
  HD62.38.B37 1999
  658'.041—dc21   98-55222
                                                                                              CIP

All rights reserved. No portion of this book may be reproduced in any form without the written permission o f the Publisher.

Printed in the United States of America.

    99   00   01   02   03 04 / BP /   10   9   8   7   6   5   4   3   2   1

It is an honor to dedicate this book to the many women who have chosen to have a home-based business, and to my dear friend for many years, Sheri Torelli. She took her family and career seriously enough to make it work. She has become very successful in her typing and computer business. She has truly been a woman with a teachable spirit.

We want to share what we've learned with all of you so one day you too can have a successful home-based business.

Emilie

This book is lovingly dedicated to my best friend, encourager, and the love of my life, Tim, and our two children, Nick and Terra—the main reasons I started working at home!

Sheri

Acknowledgments

This book is an example of many people who believed enough in their vision to step out and help others return to their homes and to start home-based businesses. My Bob has encouraged and supported me from the very beginning, over twenty years ago, when I started "More Hours In My Day" in our living room. He has always said, "You want to be good to your wife because one day she might be your boss." However, it hasn't been like that for us. We have complemented each other with our gifts and talents. Where I am weak, he is strong, and where he is weak, I am strong. We lift each other up with encouragement. We have learned to step in to get the job done with a happy smile and a grateful spirit.

We thank God for all that He has given us as we continue to step out in faith as our home-based business continues to grow.

Emilie

God blesses our commitment to Him and gives us the desires of our hearts. This book would not be possible without input and encouragement from Bob and Emilie Barnes. God blessed me when I was introduced to them and their wonderful ministry, More Hours In My Day. Their love and support over the years will never be forgotten.

There are so many special friends and family members who have encouraged me in this writing project. A special thanks to my Aunt Pat, my nephew Brad, my very special friend Lisa Sellers, the gang at Let's Network, and my "Desert Buddies" in WDW. Your support and encouragement are very much appreciated!

Sheri

Contents

From Emilie's Heart

When I was 11 years old I had my own organized home business. I sold my outgrown clothes for 25 cents each. My friends loved it! I've sold Tupperware, food supplements, jewelry, cleaning products, magazines, clothing, toys—you name it, I've sold it. Now, years later, I find myself in a home business which is very active. My Bob and I have written more than 50 books with well over three million in print. We travel most weekends doing "More Hours In My Day" seminars for women who are eager to get organized and learn how to use a feather duster, promote sound and happy values, and juggle home, work, and family.

Now with grown children and grandchildren, we have been through every aspect of building a home-based business.

I met Sheri Torelli 20 years ago. Not only have we been friends, but she has typed almost all of our manuscripts over the years as well as other projects generated with More Hours In My Day. Sheri held several secretarial jobs before her children were born and longed to work from home where she could raise her children. She worked at her typing business part-time and worked different secretarial jobs for a while. I encouraged and even begged her to devote her energy and time to making her at-home typing business successful on a full-time basis so she could be home with her children. Needless to say Sheri's job has far surpassed her dreams and expectations. God honored her heart and blessed her with a happy home, a happy husband, happy grown children, and a great home-based business.

It is an honor for me to have Sheri be a very big part of writing this book.

—Emilie

From Sheri's Heart

In the winter of 1979, I was working part-time as a church secretary and had taken some typed work to a nearby copy center. As I waited in line for service, the man behind me tapped me on the shoulder and asked how much it would cost to have something typed. I didn't have a clue how to answer his question; however, it started my entrepreneurial wheels turning.

Back at the office I told my coworker Marilyn what had happened. I told her how I wished I could type at home to make some extra money and keep doing what I loved—typing. I was also pregnant with our first child, and I really wanted to stay at home after the baby was born.

Several weeks later Marilyn came to work very excited. She had gone to work out at a local gym and met a woman who owned a home-based typing service. The lady told Marilyn she would be happy to talk to me and give me some pointers. I couldn't wait to get home and tell my husband, Tim. He was as excited as I was (maybe more) and asked me to call Natalie as soon as possible. I found out that she owned a home-based business called A-1 Typing and Resumes. She completely supported herself with her business and gave me some great tips and ideas on how to get started. I decided then that if I was able to start a business from home and it became successful, I would be willing to help anyone who wanted or needed help starting their own business.

Not long after talking to Natalie, I attended a training seminar in Northern California. While I was gone, Tim turned our spare bedroom into my new office. I came home and found my dream office with everything in place—a desk and chair, typing table, bookcase, special lighting, and even some plants to make it comfortable and appealing. And Accu-Pro Typing Service was born.

I must confess that I started my business with grandiose dreams. I figured that during the hours my son slept I would concentrate on my typing. Boy, was I in for a surprise! You can tell that these were the thoughts of a brand-new young mother. I soon discovered that when my baby slept, so did I!

In those harried early days of my fledgling business, I happened to notice a sign as I entered my church one Sunday morning. It read...

WOULD YOU LIKE TO HAVE
MORE HOURS IN YOUR DAY?

With a small, nine-month-old baby and a new business, I was feeling somewhat overwhelmed. I took one look at the sign and signed up for the seminar. I listened, took notes, and devoured everything Emilie Barnes had to say.

I had never been very organized and the idea that Emilie's system could work so encouraged me. After the seminar, I went up to speak with Emilie and discovered that her daughter, Jenny, had gone to school with my sisters and me. In the course of our conversation I told her about my new home-based business. She was very encouraging and so I boldly told her that if she ever needed to have any typing done, to let me know.

About this same time More Hours In My Day was taking off. Emilie called and asked me to help collate her organizational notebooks. I also traveled with her to her seminars, handled registration, folded boxes, worked the book table, and listened more as she talked about organization. I discovered a very basic and simple principle—organization is the key to success. Emilie presented her ideas from a biblical perspective and with tender loving concern for women and their families.

That was nearly 20 years ago. Bob and Emilie were my first "real" customers and I have counted myself fortunate to have had the privilege of typing their manuscripts and all the other typing that surrounds the success of More Hours In My Day.

I've also been privileged to work with businesspeople, attorneys, professors, and writers as my business has grown. Today, countless women call me and ask how they can start a business from their home. They are desperate to be stay-at-home moms. They are tired of the rat race and trying to be super-mom. They are willing to sacrifice some of the "extras" to be at home. And fortunately for them, working at home isn't the sacrifice that it used to be. Conservative statistics show that the average home-based business owner earns an annual salary of $25,000–$50,000. It does take time to establish your business, but the money is there.

I can think of no greater satisfaction in life than being able to take care of our children as God designed, molding them to love and serve God and readying them for responsible adulthood.

—Sheri

Introduction

Some of you may be wondering, "Why another book on home-based business organization?" I hope you will read a little further and see what will be different about this book. This book is written primarily for women who desire to return home from the workplace to raise their children. They have found that having relatives, friends, or day care centers responsible for raising and nurturing their children is not what they want. And they are choosing to make the necessary lifestyle changes to make this possible.

What makes this book unique is that we understand the need to provide necessary income for the family that sometimes is not possible with only one parent working. However, first and foremost, we feel that earning an additional income is secondary to caring for and raising our children. We are in a crisis in this country and many of our "ills" can be traced to the decline of the family. We live in a time of blended families (a term practically unheard of in the '50s), skyrocketing divorce rates, teen pregnancies, rampant drug use among teenagers, suicide, and extreme violence. One of the ways we can make a difference in our culture is to get our priorities back in order and understand that raising children is the most rewarding career we women can have.

We do believe, however, that you can use your creative abilities and supplement your family income. Doing this takes the pressure off the primary wage earner (usually dad) and allows for a more harmonious family. What we are suggesting is that you use what you know and love and turn it into a way to earn money. We are not suggesting that you trade in an office setting simply to move home with the same crazy hours and deadlines and once again neglect your primary responsibilities. Instead, we are suggesting that you take into consideration the ages of your children, then combine your skills and abilities and turn them into an enjoyable way to make some extra money.

The key to combining the job of mothering with running a successful home-based business is to first get your priorities in order. Once you have determined your priorities, then you need to get organized. Organization is the cornerstone to being successful. It is impossible to determine just how much time we lose because of disorganization, but we know that 85% of our stress comes from disorganization. We believe there are levels of organization and each woman must find the level at which she is comfortable. This is something that must be decided between both the husband and the wife. Organization can be done a little bit at a time. It doesn't have to happen all at once. But you will be surprised to see how much you can accomplish with a small amount of time each day devoted to organization. That is primarily what this book is about.

Our desire is to help you organize your home and your business. No successful home-based business will be effective if your home is disorganized. In each chapter we will offer you quick tips for organization and success stories from women who have moved home to live, love, and work all under the same roof.

What Is a Home-Based Business?

Although the definition of a home-based business varies, the most accurate description we have found is this: If you work from your home at least five hours a week, you qualify as having an official home-based business.

Working from home is the rage of the '90s and will continue into the new millennium. Yet home-based businesses are far from new. We Americans have a strong cultural tradition of working from home. Paul Revere, like many during his time, operated his silversmithing business in front of his home in Boston. And what better example of home-based business than the farmer? Until the recent advances in technology and machinery, the farm truly was one of the most steadfast of home-based businesses. There are stories after stories of generations of families involved in farming. Many of my (Sheri) relatives continue to farm in the South on land that has been in the family for several generations. This country's historical roots and present-day technology have combined to create a home-based business revolution.

It is estimated that over 70 million home-based businesses currently exist in the United States alone, and that number is expected to continue to climb at a rapid rate. By the year 2000 it is estimated that over 100 million home-based businesses will be in operation.

When I (Sheri) started my typing business in 1979, home-based businesses were rare. If you were operating a business from your home it was assumed that you were not successful enough to hold a position in an office setting. Thankfully, that has changed. Home-based businesses are now a legitimate, profitable way to earn an income—and stay at home with your kids!

Chapter
One

The Organization Test

So how organized are you? It might be easier for us to get an honest answer if we asked your spouse or your children or your boss. Whether you are currently contemplating starting a business from home or are already a seasoned home-based business veteran, it's never too late to get organized. By allotting just 15–30 minutes a day to organizing your home and office, you will be amazed at how quickly things begin to take shape.

Although two of the most ideal advantages of working from home are freedom and flexibility, once a woman realizes the total freedom of owning her own home-based business, she might confess something like this:

Take 15 minutes at the end of each day and make a "to do" list in your planner. Write down the items that need to be done the next day. As you start fresh tomorrow you will already have completed the most difficult job of the day—prioritizing your activities.

"I am completely overwhelmed with the paperwork! It is closing in on me. I am getting less done and taking more time to do it. I can't find anything and the paper monster is taking over my home. I am even more unavailable for my family than when I was working away from home."

After experiencing the reality of living and working at home, some women move back to an office setting in order to get control of their working lives. People who find success in their home-based businesses have learned to create a system for managing their homes and their work. With a system custom-made to your priorities, goals, needs, and values, you can get both your home and your home office organized and keep them that way.

In order to be completely successful, you must have a handle on the organization of your home first and then your home office. Organization isn't difficult; it's simply a matter of choosing a plan and sticking to it.

Just what is organization? Take this simple test to help you determine your level of organization and how much work you have ahead of you:

1. At this moment do you know where your car keys are?

2. Could you find your most recent tax returns in five minutes or less?

3. Do you know where your children's birth certificates and shot records are?

4. Could you find a receipt for office supplies purchased two months ago?

5. Is the sink free of dirty dishes?

6. Do you have more than three piles of paper anywhere in your home/office?

7. Could you at a quick glance give me a subtotal of revenue receipts for the previous month for your business?

8. Do you have a current list of customer names and phone numbers and could you retrieve it in under three minutes?

9. Have your bills for the month all been paid on time?

10. Do you open and sort your mail the day it arrives?

Eight or more "yes" answers – You are very organized.
Six to eight "yes" answers – You could use a tune-up.
Four to six "yes" answers – It's a jungle in there.
Less than four "yes" answers – You need a complete overhaul.

A client of mine (Sheri's) had a very exciting and successful home-based business which included a great deal of paperwork, but she was being swallowed up by clutter. She barely had any walking room left in her entire house. A small path led from the front door to her office with another path leading to the dining room and yet another path leading to the back bedrooms. She became so overwhelmed by the clutter and mess that she began to lose business and eventually closed down altogether. She was stressed to the point of exhaustion. Her problems could have been easily prevented if she had learned some very basic organizational principles:

- ✤ Do it now.
- ✤ Don't put it down, put it away.
- ✤ A place for everything and everything in its place.
- ✤ To fail to plan is to plan to fail.

Webster's definition of organization is simple: "To arrange in an orderly way; to set oneself into an orderly state of mind." We need to arrange our homes and offices in an orderly fashion to make our work productive. We will accomplish much more if we are organized. But remember—organization means different things to different people. For some it means absolutely no clutter anywhere—no piles, no excess paper. For another person it may mean having *neat* piles. Their closets and drawers are organized and labeled. They do not keep any clutter on countertops and they generally are not collectors of knick-knacks. For others organization means that drawers are neat and items easy to locate, countertops are clean but neatly displayed with decorative items, and their knick-knack collection is dusted. Depending on your personality type, organization may mean something different for you. After all, how boring it would be if we all were exactly the same! Our differences make life fun and exciting and we can be organized to fit our lifestyles.

According to Paul and Sarah Edwards, home-based business experts, it is possible for anyone to become a self-organizer. The Edwards' have spoken to hundreds of people about how they organized their work at home. They found that people are either "conventional organizers" or "unconventional organizers." The conventional organizers design strict schedules and adhere to them consistently. The unconventional organizers have the appearance of being unorganized at times, but upon closer examination are found to be extremely organized. Their organizational systems are very complex, sometimes even more complex than the conventionally organized individuals. For example, conventional organizers might use complex planners and tickler files. Unconventional organizers may use simple to-do lists and unique filing systems using binders rather than traditional file folders.

Whether their systems were conventional or unconventional, the self-organizers that the Edwards' spoke with shared these characteristics:

1. **People who are organized realize they can be in charge of how they do things.** Self-organizers have discovered that even if it doesn't seem so, they're free to choose how they're going to do things. Also, they are willing to live with the consequences of their choices. Often self-organizers only gain this wisdom after they start working from home.

2. **Self-organizers keep their priorities in mind and orchestrate their work around these goals.** Knowing what's really important to them pervades everything self-organizers do, from the hours they spend working to their choice of tasks.

3. **Self-organizers take responsibility for what happens in their work.** Since they realize that they can usually structure their work the way they want, self-organizers have also learned that they're responsible for whatever results they get. If they aren't getting what they want, they realize it's because their approach isn't

working. They take responsibility for problems as well as solutions.

4. **Although self-organizers often don't realize it, they have made a habit of following the basic principles of good systems organization.** Natural self-organizers have learned the principles of good systems organization by osmosis. They picked it up from their parents, a teacher, or on the job. The most common way people learn organizing habits is from the way they were taught to clean up their rooms as young children.

If you weren't blessed during childhood with learning the basic skills for creating and using organizational systems, don't despair. There's no need to struggle through the hazards of learning by trial and error.[1] You can use the principles in our book to design an organizational plan that will work for your home and office.

Wouldn't it be wonderful if you could wake up in the morning and know exactly where you are going, why you are going, and how to get there? Do you wish you had the secret to spending more time with your husband and children? We're here to tell you that you *can* go to bed at night and have the satisfaction of knowing

Set a goal to do one necessary but difficult chore each day. You'll have a sense of satisfaction each time you complete the task.

you have accomplished all you set out to accomplish that morning, both in your family life and in your work life. So get ready for some exciting challenges and the ride of a lifetime as we work together to become all God has designed us to become!

The Importance
of Mommy

I (Sheri) recall with fondness a very special morning with my daughter. I got up early to prepare a special tea party for Terra—a tradition we started for the first day of school. After getting dressed and having my quiet time, I set everything up in our dining area—candles, a pretty centerpiece, my best china and crystal, cute napkins, and a special treat to eat. Terra is usually an early riser like me, but when I went to wake her up she was still asleep. I quietly crept into her room and gently called her name. I told her to come to the dining room as quickly as possible. She arrived to find that I had written out a heart-felt "I Love You Because…" card and placed it on her plate. We shared

*Being a
wife and mother
is a gift.
Every woman
should realize
that she has the
greatest profession
in the
whole wide world.*

some tender moments together. I prayed for her first day at school and asked God to bless her efforts and thanked Him for giving me such a precious child. Soon Terra was off to shower and get dressed. For the next couple of days she would spontaneously hug me and thank me for making her first day of school so special. It really was a small effort on my part, but it reaped incredible rewards. My daughter knew that she was a priority to me and that even though I had a busy day planned, she was the focus for a precious few minutes.

I (Emilie) have spent similar times with my granddaughter, Christine. We are kindred spirits who bonded when she was an infant—my first grandbaby. Our relationship has been special ever since, and tea parties together have always been part of that close relationship. What a delightful experience for both of us—just two people who love each other sharing our lives over a cup of tea!

Connection with our kids happens when we devote time to them on a regular basis. Nothing can substitute for time. For those of us whose children are out or nearly out of the nest, we know all too well how quickly the years pass by. It seems that you wake up one morning and your children are grown. When they are young, you can hardly wait until they can walk, talk, potty, dress, and feed themselves. When they're older, you would give anything to have that sweet toddler back again for a week. Each age brings its own challenges and rewards. Each is unique and special. But devoting time to your children takes planning and organization. It won't happen by accident. You must be willing to make your children your priority and give them individual time with you. Nothing can replace the hours spent on the ballpark bench cheering at your son's Little League games. Beaming with pride at your daughter's play performance is a priceless memory. And what price tag can be put on children? Jobs come and go, careers change and evolve, companies merge and employees are transferred. But children are gifts to be forever treasured.

Recently on the syndicated radio talk show "Dr. Laura," one of Dr. Laura Schlessinger's listeners faxed her a poignant letter about this concept of time and priorities. After listening to Dr. Laura's program for several months, this woman decided to make the choice to come home and be there for her children. She didn't see how she could do it financially, but she knew it was the right thing for her family. What finally made her decide to quit and come home? On a particularly harried morning when she was leaving for work, her young daughter came up to her as she was walking out the door and said, "Mommy, can I please just sit on your lap for five minutes?" It broke the woman's heart and she decided that no amount of money or toys or material things could replace the needs of her children. She realized sooner rather than later that nothing can replace the importance of Mom. Regrets are realizations that come too late.

Back in the late 1980s, both of us were discussing women and their roles. I (Sheri) was a young wife and mother who was concerned about what I was seeing happen to the roles of wife and mother. Based on my talks with women all over the country, I (Emilie) predicted that we were going to see a change in women's roles in the '90s. No more supermom. Women would be sick and tired of the rat race. They couldn't possibly do it all and do a good job when they were so stretched and exhausted that they fell asleep waiting for a street light to change! Our conclusions were absolutely right. We have learned that each of us has the same 24 hours in the day. What we do with it is what separates us from one another.

We are fighting an insidious battle in our country today—the disintegration of the family. We are being hit from all sides. Divorce is at an all-time high, blended families are the norm, and child violence is on the rise. Mothers working outside the home are typical. Day care and after-school care centers have waiting lists—some several *years* long. Like no other time in history, mothers are abandoning their children so that they can "find themselves" or "experience success." And if that isn't enough, we now have those who would seek to absolve parents, particularly mothers, of any responsibility for how they parent. In her book, *The Nurture Assumption: Why Children Turn Out the Way They Do; Parents Matter Less Than You Think and Peers Matter More,* Judith Rich Harris has ignited controversy by stating "that what influences children's development...is the way their parents bring them up...is wrong." She believes that the only real contribution that parents make is providing the egg and sperm. After that nothing parents do in either a negative or positive manner makes any difference whatever as to what kind of adult the child becomes.[2] What concerns us most is that Rich Harris has a following of highly educated psychologists, doctors, and executives. She has become part of a growing backlash against the idea that parents can mold their children.

If we buy into this nonsense, then we must take a long, hard look at why we decided to become parents in the first place. Many of our qualities and characteristics—some good, some bad—can be traced directly to our parents. We have many of their inherited qualities (genes), but we have many more learned characteristics (behaviors). The key for parents is to maximize the positive qualities and minimize the negative. How we behave, how we treat others, and even how we act as wives and mothers are directly traceable to what we observed in our parents as we grew up.

My (Sheri's) husband was raised by his stepdad from the age of seven. Many of his traits can be traced directly to his stepdad and genetics had very little to do with it. He learned by observation and was definitely influenced by his environment.

How Important Is Mom As Caretaker?

The moment my (Sheri's) son, Nick, was born I knew I didn't want to leave him in day care. I wanted to be there to share in all his "firsts." Many women justify working outside the home by having a mom, an aunt, or a close family friend watch the child. *You can hire cleaners, cooks, drivers, and sitters at some hourly rate, but you can't hire the caring, compassion, and devotion of a mother at any price.*[3] We are going to make an extremely bold statement at this point: ***No one will ever care for and love and nurture your child like you.*** No one. This is a strong statement, but we believe with all our heart that Mom is best qualified to raise her children. Mom knows what makes them happy, and most of the time she knows what is wrong when they cry. Even when they are teenagers, Mom still knows her children best. When my (Sheri's) daughter, Terra, quietly comes home from school and quickly escapes to her room, I know she has probably had a fight with a friend. When she comes home her usual bubbly self, I know that her day went well with her friends as well as her teachers.

We realize that there are circumstances that make staying at home impossible for some dedicated parents, especially single parents. But these reasons for working are very different from the mother who works for emotional gratification or to buy extravagant "extras," or to feed her shopping habit. Our priorities must be in order. Day care centers and preschools are no replacement for the nurturing, love, and devotion that Mom provides. No day care center or preschool will ever be able to give the one-on-one care to your child that you can.

> "Mom!" The word stabs at me even after I have driven away from the city's finest day care center. All the teachers have college degrees and are certified in kindness. The rooms are bright, the children diverse, the groups small, and the educational content stimulating. Yet as I walk out of the place, something in my heart cries out, wailing.[4]

As women, we need to begin realizing our value as wives and mothers. There is no finer calling. Much is written in the Bible regarding the role of the mother. This role was widely accepted in the late 1950s and early 1960s. Women knew what they were supposed to do. Men worked and provided the paycheck, and women ran the home. The roles were clear and well-defined. This is no longer true. What was expected and taken for granted in that era is looked down upon today. The value of the mother's role has diminished.

More than any other single factor in the last several decades, the feminist movement of the sixties and seventies weakened the perceived value of stay-at-home moms and promoted the ideal of a working woman's worth. This concept meshed perfectly with the liberal agenda of devaluing the family unit in general. Feminists presented stay-at-home moms as the equivalent of an oppressed minority.[5]

We are happy to report that it appears the trend is changing. The husband is beginning to see the benefits of Mom staying at home, and he is becoming an encourager of her. He realizes that he is accountable for his family and their accomplishments. He sees the value of his wife's interaction with the children and the sense of security she brings to the home. What was taken for granted in the '50s and '60s is now becoming something of value.

As makers of our homes we women possess many different qualities. If you are effectively running a home, you are using talents and qualities you might never have the opportunity to use working outside your home. You now have the freedom to

Unclutter your life by saying no to good things and saying yes to the best things in life.
Live a balanced life.
Make time for yourself and your family.
Stop go-go-going.
Be a person of being rather than a person of doing.

be as creative as you like. When I (Sheri) started working at home, I was confident in my abilities both as a mother and a businesswoman. I felt far more liberated than my counterparts who worked away from home. I had no limitations on what I could achieve and accomplish. The sky was the limit!

You now have an excellent opportunity to take what you like and know how to do and make money doing it at home. This is truly the best of both worlds. You will have the desired time with your children as well as a chance to explore your creative side.

Ask yourself how you would like to be remembered by your children. Do you want to be the one who instills your value system and beliefs in them, or do you want the preschool worker, neighbor, or someone else to do it for you?

> Positive self-worth and godly character are very important to your children. Maybe they will get this outside the home, but are you willing to take the chance? Your children only have one childhood and you only get one chance.[6]

For those of us who have already watched our children go through several stages of childhood and adolescence, we know all too well how quickly they grow up. We are given such a short time with our children to mold them into responsible, well-adjusted individuals who love and serve God and are ready to face the real world. There is no finer calling than helping them to grow. The joys and trials of each age disappear in a moment and all of a sudden you wonder where the time has gone. At times it seems as though they will stay babies or toddlers forever, that you will never get a complete night's rest or a night out with your husband. But remember what older, wiser mothers have said. Enjoy these precious moments with your babies.

My sister was given a cross-stitch pattern adorned with a very thought-provoking message:

> *Cleaning and scrubbing*
> *can wait 'til tomorrow*
> *Children grow up...*
> *we've learned to our sorrow.*
> *So stay away cobwebs*
> *and dust go to sleep,*
> *I'm rocking my baby*
> *and babies don't keep!*

How true! It seems like just yesterday that our children were babies. Be thankful that God has given you the talents to enrich your family. Start today and begin to see the incredible value and worth of your role as mother!

Chapter
Three

Determine
Your Plan

Before you can begin thinking about working from home, you and your spouse must determine definite goals and priorities for your family. The cornerstone to successfully working from home is having a plan and sticking to it. As the old saying goes, "To fail to plan is to plan to fail." This applies to almost every area of our lives, but it especially applies to living and working under the same roof. Just as an architect has a plan before he starts to build a home, we must have a plan for what we want to accomplish in our families before we launch our at-home businesses.

When I (Sheri) met my husband, Tim, I was amazed and delighted with how at just 18 years of age he had mapped out such a detailed plan for his life. He had developed short- and long-term goals for the next 10 years. I, on the other hand, wasn't sure what I was doing the next 10 days! Tim told me he wanted to have a car, a house, and a boat before he married. He saved his money and spent wisely. Fortunately, as life's circumstances changed, he decided to alter his goals a little and marry me instead of buying the boat!

As a result of his planning and goal-setting, Tim bought his first house when he was 19. He bought the house before he purchased a car. Although I struggled with setting goals, as Tim began reaching his I could tangibly see the value of setting goals and working hard to accomplish them. It didn't happen overnight and it wasn't easy, but I learned that anything worth having was worth whatever effort it took to achieve it.

Over the years that Tim and I dated, we discovered that our value systems were the same. We shared the same feelings about our relationship to God and our spiritual beliefs, the way we would raise our children, and how we would handle our finances. Because of this, I was confident that determining priorities and setting goals would come with time.

Set short-range goals that build toward your long-range purpose.

The Big Picture

One of the greatest helps for effective family planning and prioritizing is developing a "family ideal" or mission statement. This means deciding the main purpose for your family and stating it in a single sentence or two. A family ideal that serves as the basis for your life should be determined early. And while our value system doesn't change, the family ideal and the goals and priorities that go along with it may change—sometimes several times. It helps you begin to realize why you do what you do. Please note that it doesn't matter if you've been married for a number of years and have never had a mission statement—it is never too late to develop one.

Because our relationship with God is the cornerstone of my (Sheri's) family, we wanted a family ideal that had its basis in the Bible. And I would like to point out that we did not have a family ideal until after we had been married for a number of years. We prayed about it and searched through the Bible and came up with a verse in 1 Thessalonians (5:15b) which says, "...but always seek after that which is good for one another and for all men." Tim and I have always been a couple with a deep desire to help other people. We like to give to people and see them succeed, and we have handed down this trait to our son and daughter. Children learn what they live and what they see their parents do. As a result, Nick and Terra are very aware of others and their needs and enjoy lending a helping hand.

In deciding on your family ideal you must evaluate your values and beliefs. Your family ideal must be consistent with these two aspects or else you will continually have conflict in verbalizing exactly what you want out of life. When your actions, based on your goals, are in harmony with your values you will experience balance, a sense of security, and gratification. However, when you are out of balance with your value system, you will experience frustration and guilt.

My Bob and I (Emilie) selected a Purpose of Life statement or family ideal to reflect our values and beliefs and give us a sense of balance. We have adopted Matthew 6:33 as our mission statement: "...seek first His kingdom and His righteousness; and all these things shall be added to you." This verse exemplifies our lifestyle and manner of doing our work. It has been a tremendous help as we minister through More Hours In My Day. We spend time evaluating our effectiveness in relation to our mission statement and reevaluate it when necessary.

Your family ideal may change over time and need to be restated several times throughout your lifetime. Because it serves as a guideline for family and business decisions you will make, it is very important to carefully choose the ideal you will use for your family. Spend time praying and searching for a statement that reflects all you are and all you hope to accomplish.

Priorities and Goals

Nothing is more critical to the success of your home and family than a carefully thought-out list of priorities and goals. Priorities help us determine what goals we will adopt. Depending on your personality, your list may be very simple or, if you are more detail-oriented like we are, your list may be more complex.

My (Emilie's) husband, Bob, states that goals are "dreams with a deadline." This is a great definition that is easy to understand. A goal needs to be written out, and it must include the quantity and a specific deadline. The family priorities and goals need to be specifically for the family. In a later chapter we will examine the home business goals. Because we have determined that our family is the first priority with the business second, we need to look at the family priorities and goals first.

Because God created men and women with differences, we also believe that goals will be stated differently by both husband and wife. It's important for Tim and me (Sheri) to write our goals separately and then discuss them together in order to come up with one set of goals that reflects both our ideals. I suggest that once you write out your individual goals, take an evening together someplace away from home and spend time discussing and evaluating the goals and just enjoying the time together. This time is always a chance for Tim and me to reflect on our early days of marriage and how we have changed and grown. Not only do we enjoy an evening out together, we also accomplish an otherwise tedious task.

If you're new to setting goals and determining priorities, don't despair. You may want to start off with short segments of time such as goal setting for the next six months instead of tackling the next 10 years.

Our (Tim and Sheri's) goal-setting priorities are very simple and once again based in God's Word.

Studies show that the success rate for people who write down their goals is about 90 times greater than for those who don't.

1. *Relationship to God — Matthew 6:33*

My personal quiet time is very special to me and I treasure the moments I spend with Jesus. Because I am a morning person, I start my day by communing with the Lord. I spend time alone in my backyard just after it gets light outside and read and meditate on God's Word. What a special time this is for me. Once I have completed my reading and meditation, I come in to a quiet place in my home and kneel for a season of prayer. This starts my day off right. I have entrusted my goals and desires to what God wants me to accomplish and trust that He is in control of my day. I have given him "my" list of what needs to be accomplished and have asked His guidance for what He would have planned for me as I prepare for another day with my family and my business.

2. *Spouse — Proverbs 12:4*

My husband is my next priority. Emilie has told me many times that it is very important to remember that I was a wife to my husband *before* I was a mother to my children. My husband has a special place in my heart and he knows it. I often tell people that next to my relationship with Jesus, Tim is the most important person to me. Because he is a firefighter he can spend several days at a time at home with me. He is also gone for 24-hour periods. I have learned to make the most of this unusual schedule by making Tim my priority on the days he is home. I schedule time with friends and special "dates" with our kids when he is working. Tim knows he is important to me, and I work hard at keeping him a priority. Another added value of working at home is that when your husband is there, so are you!

3. *Children — Psalm 127:3*

Children are truly a gift from God! I have two teenagers, Nick and Terra. My son is 18 years old and my daughter is 16½. They are each so unique and special. It is vital that they know just what they mean to me. I try to demonstrate my love and devotion to them by being there for them. No toy or game or outing can replace our time spent together. They're not perfect and neither am I, but we love to spend time together talking and sharing. My days with the children at home are quickly passing. Nick is in college and will soon be moving away. Terra is a junior in high school. I have incredible treasured memories and I can say with pride that I have been able to be at home with my children through all the seasons of their lives.

4. *Home — Proverbs 31:27*

This is where home organization comes into place. You will never be completely successful running a business out of your home if your house is a complete mess. Organization is the key to being successful. This is true of most areas of our lives. In a later chapter I will share with you the most effective way to clean and organize your home. Emilie's "Total Mess to Total Rest" plan is absolutely the ideal way to finally get a handle on your clutter.

↬ Business at home: This is where your business fits in the order of priorities. You will notice that it is not first or second or third. You will have to work very hard to keep your business in its proper order of priority.

5. *Yourself — Matthew 19:19*

This area is a struggle for many women. But if we are going to give our best to our husbands, our children, and our friends, we must take time to regroup and refresh. This can be done in a variety of ways—taking a break in the afternoon for a cup of tea or coffee, enjoying a nice hot bath, going shopping with a friend, taking a long walk. The list is endless. Do what makes you really happy. I am a rubber stamp-aholic. I collect stamps and make cards for friends. I also like to go out for coffee with a friend or my husband. When I feel refreshed, it shows in my attitude and what I am able to accomplish.

6. *Outside the Home — Matthew 28:19*

⊹ Church: Unfortunately, this priority usually gets re-routed to the top of the list. We confuse our relationship to God with church ministry. Please don't misunderstand. I believe that church attendance and worship are vital to our Christian walk, but too many times "ministry" gets clouded and our husband and children take a much lower priority than God intended for them to take. Good planning will help you make the most of your gifts, and you'll discover how God can help you use them in your church.

⊹ School: If you have school-aged children, you need to be available to volunteer occasionally at their school. This gives you a chance to demonstrate to your kids that they are important to you and that you can make time for them.

⊹ Community: This is the area that most relates to our businesses. I serve on a home-based business committee with our local Chamber of Commerce. We work to change the local ordinances for home-based businesses. I also work for several organizations in a volunteer capacity. These are important to my business as they enhance my visibility in the community. However, once again remember to keep the outside activities to a minimum and within the guidelines you have set up for your family.

A motto I often use is, "You always have time for the things you put first; you seldom have time for the things you put last." If we determine that our priorities are important and worthwhile, then we will seek to fulfill those priorities.

It is important to start the day off with a list of appointments and family obligations that has been prepared the previous evening. In a later chapter we will discuss the importance of calendaring and how to make the most of this helpful tool.

Conflicts between commitments will arise on occasion, but with a good plan and our priorities in order they can be resolved quickly. Remember, conflict can be good if it forces us to become more organized. Organization is the key to making everything work together. There will be times when family and home business obligations will conflict and changes may need to be made. If you focus on the positive, you can make realistic changes that will enhance your family as well as your home-based business.

Remember that your goal is to get organized so that you can work toward your mission or purpose in life.

HOMEwork

Provide yourself with a notebook planner, either looseleaf or spiral-bound, that is small enough to carry around with you. This planner will become your "master list"—a single continuous list that replaces all the small slips of paper you've been using. Use the planner to keep track of all errands to run, things to do or buy, and general notes to yourself about anything that will require action.

A Hobby Turns into a Business

The Bluma Family

Greg, Teresa, and sons John and James

Busy and active parents, husband Greg is a fire engineer with the city fire department and wife Teresa has a bachelor of science degree in public administration. Up until 1997, Teresa worked for the City of Riverside as a senior administrative analyst for Riverside's municipal utility, and was responsible for the utility's legislative and intergovernmental affairs. The job was challenging and financially rewarding, but the long hours and required travel were difficult on the family.

In 1990 the Blumas discovered that their youngest son, James, was moderately retarded and would need special care and attention. Greg and Teresa dedicated themselves to helping James get the best upbringing, medical attention, and education available. The family kept plugging away, always pondering the benefits of having Teresa stay at home, perhaps working at a home-based family business. However, change was a risky thing, and the family decided not to take any giant steps until 1997.

In 1993 the Blumas took up the "hobby" of working with search and rescue dogs. Both Greg and Teresa worked with separate dogs, and with some perseverance they certified their dogs through the California Office of Emergency Services and the Federal Emergency Management Agency. Teresa's passion for working with dogs was especially evident. She'd spent time working under different trainers and was acquiring the knowledge necessary to take the next step.

In 1996 Greg and Teresa purchased a kennel on an acre of land and K-9 Specialists, as the business came to be called, was born. At first Teresa retained her position with the City and worked with the dogs as time would allow. Yet eventually the Blumas decided that their family's needs could be better met if Teresa stayed at home and worked at the kennel. The loss of her steady paycheck was a major concern, but they believed that with enough hard work and dedication, the needs of the family—including the financial needs—would be met.

Today, Teresa trains dogs in a variety of disciplines, including family and service dogs. She also trains dogs for the deaf and certifies other service dogs. In addition, she is an explosives detection dog handler and works many details for high-profile individuals and families. Recently, Teresa started a new business venture called Detection Dogs, Ltd., where she and her partner are available with narcotics detection dogs for use in private homes, schools, or businesses. Detection Dogs also provides weapons detection dogs (for firearms) upon request.

K-9 Specialties provides a nice supplement to the Bluma family's income, and the business continues to grow beyond their expectations. Greg is a great help with the business, handling many of the maintenance projects. It is not the fast-paced, high-paying job that Teresa held before, but the non-financial rewards that the family has reaped are priceless. James has progressed by leaps and bounds, far beyond any hopes the family or his doctors previously had for his progress! Teresa now volunteers as a soccer referee and is there for the kids after school when they need her. Between Teresa and Greg's schedules, the Blumas rarely need day care.

Their dedication and hard work have paid off, and they wouldn't have it any other way. As the credit card commercials might say, "Kennel with house: $170,000; repainting: $1,000; bag of dog food: $30; staying home with the family: priceless."

Chapter Four

Business Goals

Once you have determined your family goals, it's time to begin thinking about goal-setting for your business. Just as a marksman must have a target to aim for, a business owner must have a plan in order to be successful. It is vitally important to remember that the business goals *must* complement the family priorities and goals. You will be most successful working at home if you remember that your family is number one. If all your decisions are made with this in mind, you will make wise choices. Otherwise, you have only managed to change your business address and not your philosophy. For example, if one of your goals as a family is to spend an evening each week playing games together, you must guard and protect that time when planning for and scheduling your business projects and appointments.

If working at home is a brand-new concept for your family, here are some guidelines that might prove helpful:

- ✦ In working at home, it is vital that you prayerfully evaluate your family priorities and goals regularly and often in the beginning. Be willing to change if necessary.

- ✦ Working from home successfully will naturally demand organization.

In my experience I (Sheri) have found that, in general, women have a better handle on how to combine the family and home with an at-home business. Men are better at goal setting and prioritizing. You can utilize these strengths to bring about harmony in the home. Because the woman is generally the heartbeat of the family, she will better know what can realistically be accomplished on a day-to-day basis. Because she was created to be a nurturer, she knows how her family thinks and feels. She understands the limits of her husband and her children.

Men are better equipped to analyze a situation, look clearly at the facts, and make decisions that will enhance the family as a whole. Men and women are different and unique by design. God understood that an effective family would need these differences that complement each other. Each spouse has both strengths and weaknesses. A wise couple will decide who is better equipped in a certain area and make the most of what God has perfectly conceived.

My husband, Tim, is an extremely decisive person. He thinks quickly and can analyze a situation immediately. He is also an exceptional businessman. He understands business and how it works. So when it comes to the management of Accu-Pro Typing, including what needs the business has and what will make the business grow, Tim's strengths in this area are far superior to mine. I willingly concede to him regarding these business decisions. However, he is well aware that I am the heartbeat of the business. Therefore, any decisions he makes are prayerfully considered, completely thought out, and thoroughly discussed with me. I know my customers well, and he understands this. I believe our partnership is one of the main reasons the business has flourished over the years. Our goal is to complement, not to compete with, each other.

Some types of businesses that operate from home will demand a more professional setting. My typing service is a business in which customers come to my home to drop off and pick up work. If your business requires that customers come to your home, you must make sure your priorities and goals allow for definite limits on time and scheduling. The amount of time you allow for appointments will depend entirely on the ages of your children and your husband's schedule. When my children were infants and very small toddlers, the time I could devote to seeing customers was very limited. As they grew, so also did the time I could devote to scheduling appointments. Remember that your business will grow and evolve as your children grow and mature.

Time and Money

If we are going to realistically determine the feasibility of coming home to raise our families and work, decisions regarding time and money become most critical. The goals you set must be realistic and practical. A good plan will ensure success. The most successful at-home businesses

Remember that setting goals and planning for those goals with realistic expectations in mind is what makes good things happen.

are businesses that make their families the first priority. We say this often because it is vital that you remember why you came home in the first place. It is very easy to start out with expectations of making your family the priority. However, once you come home and find you *can* make a great deal of money, you might become more focused on the business than on your family. We have personally seen many at-home businesses which grew so quickly that soon the business was number one and the family took a back seat. It became the same rat race as working outside the home. Money cannot be the first priority for your business—if it is, your family will suffer. Remember your original goals and priorities. An at-home business can only be considered truly successful when your family comes first.

Two Key Mistakes to Avoid

In his book *Women Leaving the Workplace,* Larry Burkett suggests that women should avoid two key mistakes when deciding to leave the workplace. His information has been compiled from thousands of women around the country who have made the choice to come home to raise their children.

Failure to Seek God's Will

Above everything else, Christians are accountable to God. God's Word says, "...keep seeking the things above, where Christ is seated at the right hand of God. Set your mind on the things above, not on the things that are on the earth" (Colossians 3:1-2).

Most Christians acknowledge that it's important to operate according to God's wisdom and His timetable. But when a mother is eager to be home with her children, this principle is easy to violate.

Failure to Get Your Husband's Approval

The vast majority of the women we surveyed said that having their husband's support was critical. Those who failed to gain this support said the resulting discontent in their marriages negated virtually all the benefits of being at home.

Staying at home will require some sacrifices, and if a husband is not willing to make those sacrifices, the resulting tension can undermine a marriage.[7]

Practical Steps to Goal-Setting

Over the years we have listened to countless stories about successful businesses and how they started. Each step of the pyramid is important. Consider all the factors and visualize victory.

Step #1—Determine the Plan

1. Prayerfully choose your family ideal or mission statement.

Prayer is the vital ingredient. God's timing is everything.

2. Determine family priorities and goals.

Keep in mind the ages of your children and your husband's busy schedule when deciding what is first priority.

3. Determine business goals.

Carefully pray about and consider your family goals when determining the goals for the business. Start out in small segments of time (six months) and work up to a 10-year plan.

Step #2—Organize

1. Organize your home.

In our opinion, this is the vital ingredient to success and the part often overlooked when women consider working at home. Your home must be organized and functioning in an orderly fashion in order for you to even consider an at-home business.

2. Organize your office.

To make the best use of your time for your business, you must have an organized work area. Remember that organization is long-term and ongoing. It doesn't happen in one day, but you can achieve it by taking daily steps in the process. Don't despair if you are basically not an organized person. Organization can be learned.

Step #3—Obtain Needed Resources

1. Gather your equipment.

First determine what you absolutely must have in order to begin working. Then make a "wish list" of items that you would like to obtain as soon as possible.

2. Find your furniture.

Once again, obtain only the necessary furniture at the beginning. Don't forget to shop yard sales and going-out-of-business sales and to scan the newspaper for inexpensive furniture someone may no longer need or wants to get rid of.

3. Stock up on supplies.

Watch advertisements for sales and specials at office supply stores. Start off with the bare necessities and add to your stock as money provides.

Step #4—Market Your Business

1. Find your customers.

For many businesses this is the most critical and difficult part. You may have a great business idea, but without clients you really have nothing. In a later chapter we will discuss tried-and-true methods of finding that elusive customer.

2. Determine you product/service pricing.

Determine what you will sell or the service you will offer. Research pricing in your area from other similar businesses.

Share your goals with people who really care about you and want to help you.

Step #5—Maintain the Balance Between the Family and the Business

1. Set your working schedule.

Determine when you will work and stick to those hours.

2. Set aside time for your husband.

This ingredient is most critical for a happy marriage. He needs to feel important and respected.

3. Set aside time for the children.

Make the children and their activities a priority as necessary. Remember that they are the reason you came home.

Step #6—Visualize Your Financial Goals and See Them Realized

1. Set realistic and obtainable goals.

Your financial goals will ensure success or failure. Prayerfully consider all factors and allow God to guide in this important area.

2. Set a goal of being in the "black" the first year.

In our experience working with hundreds of at-home businesspeople, the ones that were most successful had a goal to be making a profit the first year.

Step #7—Reevaluate Consistently

1. Evaluate those stated priorities and goals often and make changes when necessary.

Life and its circumstances will dictate the changes that are necessary to reach your goals. Don't be afraid of change.

Your business will achieve the success you desire if your family is in its proper priority. With God as the head of your home, He will give wisdom and guidance when you ask. Seek Him first. He waits with open arms to bless and give you the desires of your heart. Then get ready for the time of your life!

HOMEwork

Make a list of five business goals that you wish to attain by the end of the year, then reach them!

1.

2.

3.

4.

5.

Chapter
Five

Spousal Support

I (Sheri) remember the day I came home from work to tell Tim about my idea for an at-home typing business. Because he had always been very supportive of me and my ideas, I was sure he would at least hear me out. Even so, I wasn't sure how he would react to my leaving my job and coming home to work with so many unknowns. Besides, he was still getting used to the idea of a new baby coming soon! When we sat down to discuss my idea, he became very excited but still had many questions such as, "How much money will you be able to make?" and "What kind of equipment will we have to buy?" He listened while I gave him as much information as I had. We agreed together that I needed to do some more research before we decided that this was the right thing for us.

Today, information about home-based businesses is readily available; however, in 1979 it was very scarce. The only things I really knew were that I loved to type and that I was very good at it. In those days, very few people owned and operated businesses out of their homes and those who did were viewed with some suspicion. To get more information, I contacted the only other typing service in Riverside and was pleased that the owner, Natalie Lee, was more than delighted to talk with me. After talking with her and hearing first-hand how she supported herself with her business, Tim and I decided to take the next step.

Initially it was me who came up with the idea for the typing business, but I am here to tell you that without Tim's enthusiastic support it never would have materialized. His contributions proved invaluable. Spousal support, second only to regular prayerful consideration, is the key ingredient to success in working from home.

Over the years many women have come to me for advice on how to start a home business. The first thing I ask them is if their husbands are supportive of their working from home. If the answer is yes, then we proceed to the next step. If the answer is no, I gently try to convince them that maybe this isn't the right time to pursue their idea. To the Christian women I speak with, I tell them to make their idea a matter of prayer first before they approach their husbands. I encourage them to ask God to make their husbands receptive to a new idea and to let God begin His work.

Because we believe that men are responsible for their families, we also believe that any time you seek to begin a project such as working from home, spousal support is a must. Remember that you are a team. This isn't you against him. As you go through the process of deciding if this is right for your family, you will grow closer and communication will improve if you view this as a learning experience and not a battle. We know of several businesses where the woman went ahead on her own to start a business, only to have it fail several months down the road. Their husbands had never been behind them with support and when conflicts eventually arose, it became a battle of wills.

How can you present your idea in such a way that your husband will listen and honestly consider the possibility of your working at home? Over the years we have come up with several steps you can take to maximize the possibility of a positive response.

1. *Make your idea a matter of prayer before you approach your husband.*

Nothing can guarantee failure more quickly than neglecting to pray earnestly about your desire to come home. When we make God our priority, He gives us the desires of our heart—but in *His* timing. God can't wait to bless us, but He must have our hearts.

2. *Do your homework.*

After you have decided the type of business in which you are interested, get busy finding out everything you can about that particular business. Are there like businesses in your area? Is the market saturated? Or is there a market at all? How do like businesses charge for their goods and services? What will it cost to start up the business? Try to get the facts and just the facts. Your husband will be impressed that you are educated in what interests you.

3. *Make a list of pros and cons.*

Now that you've done your homework, make a list of the pros and cons of working at home. Be realistic and honest. This will help you, too, as you consider what is interesting to you and what you like to do.

4. *Be willing to listen to him.*

If initially your husband is inclined to say no or wait, it may be because he is looking at the bigger picture. Because husbands are generally the primary support for their families and usually are able to quickly determine if an idea has any merit, you need to be willing to listen to his side and how he feels. He really only wants what is best for you and the family. This is an excellent time for communication between the two of you. Don't forget that you are a team with both of you on the same side. Don't make it a matter of wills—ask for God's guidance and we guarantee He will provide it.

Keep in mind that the husband and wife should complement, not compete with, one another. Competition is great on the ballfield, but it can seriously damage even the strongest marriage.

*A*sk yourself, "What's the best use of my time and energy right now?" If that's not what you are doing, then switch to a higher priority. What you are doing might be good, but is it the best?

Support must be mutual and vital in creating a healthy home environment so that working from home can be possible. You will find that each of you have individual talents that will make the business successful. You may have special strengths in the area of business or marketing, while he may be extraordinarily creative. One of the best ways to gain support from your husband is to utilize his talents as much as possible. My husband, Tim, is an excellent businessman. His degree in Business Management has been so helpful to our typing business. Before becoming a firefighter, he worked for ten years as a meatcutter in retail stores. Tim understands the concept of customer service and its importance in a small business. His contributions are priceless and I truly appreciate his input. He has helped me see that change is not a bad thing and is actually vital to success.

We have told you that your husband's support is mandatory if you want to have a successful at-home business. However, there is another part to support. As a wife, you need to be supportive of your husband and his work outside the home as well as the contributions he makes to help the at-home business run smoothly. Be considerate of the time you set aside for him and assure him that the home will run efficiently. As you keep your husband a priority, he will naturally reciprocate and help you out when the need arises.

Conflicts naturally will occur, so communication will be vital to alleviating struggles when they happen. For example, as a couple you have decided that dinner needs to be served at 5:30 P.M. You have planned your meals and you are organized. However, at 4:30 P.M. you receive a frantic call from a regular customer that will require dinner be delayed a few minutes while you help this customer out of the dilemma. As a supportive team player, your husband has several options at this point: order a pizza for the family, offer to fix a simple dinner, or finish up what you have started. As long as this is a rare occurrence, he will gladly comply. He knows the importance of the business and values your customers. You are fully aware of your priorities and the importance of keeping them. Because communication is good between the two of you, you can easily come up with a viable solution. Be prepared for the unexpected, but don't allow it to become habit.

Working at home can enhance your family life and the times you share together as long as you remember your priorities and communicate regularly. On several occasions one of my customers has shown up without an appointment or arrived early. If I am away from my office, Tim will "entertain" the customer until I get back. Sometimes I will have one customer who arrives early for an appointment and one who comes in late. Throw in an unexpected customer without an appointment and I have a roomful of people waiting to be helped. Once again, Tim saves the day by offering refreshments or talking with the customers. He has had some very interesting conversations with customers and has learned a lot over the years. It adds to the sense of customer service I give my clients and they enjoy the relaxed atmosphere and conversation.

As you learn to depend on each other, you will grow stronger as a couple. You can maximize each other's strengths and minimize the weaknesses. The faith you have in one another's abilities in other areas of life will carry over into the business as well. I know Tim can easily take care of a customer if I am delayed, and I am confident in his ability to "hold down the fort" until I arrive.

Tim's support spills over into other areas, including projects that will enhance our home's appearance to my typing customers. Many a project has been started with the idea that it will be very eye-appealing to our clients. Tim works very hard at home and I appreciate every effort he makes. Because he wants to see the business succeed as much as I do, he always takes the time to hear me out and give his opinion when I consult him about purchases for the office. We discuss everything thoroughly and I depend on him to give me sound advice. I tend to be more impulsive than he is, so his ideas are very important to me. And it's comforting to know he has the family as his primary priority as he makes decisions. My confidence in Tim has grown over our years of living, loving, and working together. This is why we both stress spousal support so adamantly. It is so critical to success.

Accu-Pro Typing would still be a dream had it not been for the total support I received from Tim. Because he loved me so much, he was willing to take a chance on a business venture at a time when it was difficult to work from home. In fact, his confidence in me made me want to work that much harder to prove he was right! Over the years he has continued to build me up to friends and family. He believes in me and I have faith and trust in him. Our decision to have me come home is one we have never regretted. Now as we watch our children approach adulthood, it is with confidence and pride that we realize that in this case the end truly justified the means.

HOMEwork

Make sure that each decision you make for your business includes input from your spouse. It will make him really feel a part of what you are doing.

Chapter Six

The Meaning of Success

uccess is defined by Webster as "a favorable or satisfactory outcome or result." Many people assume without a doubt that success is essentially material and that it can be measured in money, prestige, or an abundance of material possessions. These can certainly play a role, but having such things does not provide an automatic guarantee of success. The success of our families and businesses has to be defined in many nonmaterial ways as well. It should include the ability to love and to have compassion, the capacity to be joyful and to spread that joyfulness to others, the security of knowing that one's life serves an ultimate purpose, and, lastly, a sense of connection to the Creator of the universe.

Even though most of us would like the pleasure and peace of mind that a clean, orderly home and office bring, remember that most working-at-home mothers never have their homes in perfect order.

This deeply profound sense of a spiritual dimension brings inner satisfaction and true success.

My (Sheri's) husband, Tim, has come up with a great definition of success as it relates to the family and the business at home:

> Success is not determined by the amount of money one makes, but on setting and obtaining certain goals.

Let's say, for example, that you start a business and, after prayer and planning, you decide that your goal is to earn enough money each month to make the car payment. If you reach that goal, you are successful. Some people may decide that their goal is to earn enough money to buy groceries each month. If they achieve that goal, they are successful. Success means different things to different people.

If you automatically set certain monetary goals for your business without taking all factors into consideration, you are setting yourself up for failure. By this we mean that if you decide you must make $2,000 a month and you have arrived at this decision without doing the preliminary planning, you will most likely fail.

Success is not an abstract concept. It is deliberate and well thought-out.

People who are successful visualize themselves as successful. They see the glass half-full instead of half-empty. A positive outlook can go further to determining success than just about anything. This doesn't mean the road is always easy, but positive people exude a "can-do" attitude, and attitude is a vital ingredient to success. Our attitude is the thermometer of who we really are. Attitude doesn't change when things don't go our way. A good attitude says, "Let's try a different approach." Success breeds success. Abraham Lincoln failed over 100 times in business ventures and ended up as one of our most beloved presidents. He never gave up; he kept plugging away. He believed in himself and saw himself a winner. After each failure he picked himself up and continued toward the next goal. He was truly the epitome of success.

In the early days of my at-home business, there were times when Tim and I wondered if we were doing the right thing. Remember, the things I am sharing with you in this book were learned the hard way. We had no guidelines to follow and no experts to guide us. No books were written to give us an outline for success. We depended on each other and God to see us through. The old cliché "Ignorance

Realize that you are responsible for causing your own effects in life. Tackle the toughest, most challenging assignments in your life first, understanding that your gratification will come after you have made the effort to do the job.

is bliss" was true in our case—and it probably kept us from quitting! Had we known the struggles that lay ahead, we might not have proceeded.

Thank God, He knew the bigger picture and way back then He was setting the groundwork for today. In God's timing everything is best. I would have been unable to write a book and conduct seminars and workshops 10 years ago. But for over 20 years my lifelong dream has been to write a book. God was preparing me many years ago for reaching this goal today. I will consider myself successful writing this book if one woman who reads it decides to come home to raise her children and work from home. It will have been worth every minute of writing and research. Nothing worth having comes without character-building trials and hard work. Success comes about when realistic and practical goals are set and obtained.

Celebrate your successes and always include your family in the festivities. The people you live with and care most about are your best support system. They only want to see you succeed and be happy. Make sure you take time to celebrate each goal as it is reached and thank God as He blesses your efforts.

HOMEwork

Are you a morning person or a night person? Your efficiency and success may increase if you arrange your tasks as much as possible around the natural rhythms of your body. Try scheduling top-priority projects during your peak hours and routine work during your "low" times.

Chapter
Seven

Total Mess to
Total Rest

Could you invite someone to your home or your home office and allow them to go through your closets and drawers without needing at least a week to get ready for the inspection? Most of us would have to answer no. But there is a way to get your home and office organized. As Henry Ford once said, "Nothing is particularly hard if you divide it into small jobs." This holds true in almost any area of our lives, including the organization and maintenance of our homes and offices. The key is maintenance. How many times have you gone through a room and cleaned it from top to bottom only to find it messy again in just a short time? Just cleaning and throwing things out is not enough.

Use the salami method to reach your goal. If the size of the project overwhelms you, tackle it one piece at a time. You wouldn't eat a salami whole, would you? You'd cut it into slices. Do the same thing with your big projects.

You need to have a system to keep it organized.

Organization is also a matter of attitude. You most likely will take time to complete tasks that are important to you or your husband or children. One of my (Sheri's) favorite sayings says it all, "You always have time for the things you put first, you seldom have time for the things you put last." You need to determine what "firsts" are important to you and your family. Sometimes a compromise will need to be made. Be open and communicate on a regular basis. This will eliminate resentment building up over time about something as minor as a load of laundry left unfolded.

I (Emilie) have found a tried-and-true method for cleaning and organization that has been used by thousands and thousands of women around the country. My method has made the often overwhelming job of cleaning and organization simple and easy to do. My plan is called, "Total Mess To Total Rest."

I (Sheri) found Emilie's plan to be a lifesaver when it came to home organization. It was a plan that even I could master. Emilie taught me that anyone can learn to be organized if they *want* to be organized. Remember, organization can be learned!

In this chapter we will show you how you can clean your home and office and keep them clean in just 15 minutes a day. We will show you how to take that mess, no matter how big it is, and turn it into an organized home and office that you'll be able to work and relax in. You will control your home instead of your home controlling you. This method is especially effective for organizing your home office because you will never again have to search for something simply because you cannot remember where you put it among all those piles of paper.

Equipment You'll Need

- ↦ 3 trash bags

- ↦ 6–12 "Perfect Boxes" (12"×12"×8" with a lid)

- ↦ 3"×5" card file box with tabbed dividers—10 cards in 7 different colors

- ↦ A filing cabinet (or desk drawer or a Perfect Box) and 10 colored file folders

You'll want to commit yourself to approximately five weeks to unclutter your clutter. Don't become overwhelmed thinking about it. You're

Sometimes all it takes to eliminate mess, clutter, and confusion are a few hooks here, a basket or two there, and a reshuffling of items on a shelf. Buy one small basket or plastic bin (color-code to represent the various members of your family) for each person and hang the baskets near the coat closet door. Use them for gloves, mittens, winter hats, scarves, and other small but important items.

To organize the various booklets and pamphlets that come with cooking and home-care appliances, punch holes into self-sealing plastic bags so that they will fit into a three-ring notebook. Use one bag for each appliance and seal.

going to take a small portion at a time—only one or two rooms a week for the next five weeks. You'll do it nice and slow, and you'll gradually get your entire home organized.

Your organizing can all be done in 15-minute time slots. On Monday, go into Room 1 and clean like mad for 15 minutes, then forget about it until Tuesday when you do the same thing you did Monday, spending 15 minutes cleaning and organizing. Use a timer so that you don't go past 15 minutes. It's very easy to get so involved that you forget about the time. Continue this process throughout the week. Presto! By the end of the week you will have spent one hour and 30 minutes in Room 1. You'll still have Sunday off and a nice, clean, well-organized room. Continue this process until every room in the house is complete.

Start with three large trash bags and label them "Put Away," "Throw Away," and "Give Away." Now imagine yourself standing at the front door with these three big trash bags. Ring the doorbell, then walk through the front door. The first room you come to will be the first room you're going to clean, unless it's the kitchen. (If that's the room you walk into first, move on. Save the kitchen for last because you'll need all the experience you can get before tackling it.) To make it easy, let's say we step into the living room and on our right is the hall closet. So open up the hall closet. Now take everything out of it. You have to be aggressive in deciding what to do with all the stuff you've taken out of the closet. We recommend that you call a friend who would be willing to help with your house (and you help with her house). It's great to have a friend involved because she'll help you make decisions that you haven't been able to make for years and years.

Put into the hall closet all those things that actually belong in a hall closet. These include sweaters, coats, umbrellas, books, football blankets, binoculars, tennis rackets, baseball bats, balls, etc.

By now you've probably discovered all these other things that don't belong there, such as old magazines you've collected for six or seven years. (You were going to look through them some rainy day and cut out the pictures and recipes, but you never did.) So now you have to get rid of those things. You've also been storing papers and receipts and all sorts of other things in the closet, so you'll put these either in the Put Away bag, the Throw Away bag, or the Give Away bag.

Make it a habit to return everything to its proper place and remind others to do so. If you do this daily, it takes less time than waiting until the situation is out of control. An even bigger bonus is that you needn't spend time looking for out-of-place objects.

Do small chores as the need occurs so that they occupy little time. For example, laundry left until the weekend can consume the weekend. Instead, start a load before breakfast, put it in the dryer after breakfast, and it's done.

As you go through your home every week for the next five weeks, you will begin to fill up these bags. At the end of the fifth week you may have three, ten, or fifteen bags of various things. Then you put twisties on the trash bags marked Throw Away and set them out for the garbage or recycling trucks. Now they're gone! You've got all those things out of the way.

Now you have two types of bags left: the Give Away bags and the Put Away bags. The Give Away bags will hold things that you may want to hand down to some other family member or friend, or clothing that you want to give to a thrift shop, sell at a garage or rummage sale, or donate to your church or the Salvation Army. And what do you do with the contents of the Put Away bags? Either put the items in their correct place in the house or store them in one of your Perfect Boxes. Be sure to note the box number and contents in your index file card or a "Box" file on your computer.

The next room that you need to organize before you tackle the rest of the home is your office. The same principles apply here as with the hall closet. Be ruthless and get rid of as much clutter as possible. Don't get overwhelmed, just remember to work at it a little bit at a time. You'll be surprised at how quickly the job gets done when you break it down into manageable sections.

Storage

Get your Perfect Boxes with lids and number each box. Assign each box a 3"×5" card with a corresponding number. For example:

Box 1—Baby mementos
Box 2—Toys
Box 3—Summer (or winter) clothes
Box 4—Tax information
Box 5—High school yearbooks
Box 6—Scrapbooks
Box 7—Old pictures
Box 8—Scrap fabrics
Box 25A—Christmas decorations—candles, holders, etc.
Box 25B—Christmas ornaments
Box 25C—Holiday tablecloths and napkins, poinsettia napkin rings, etc.

That's only a start; you, no doubt, have many more categories for storage. But you're not done yet. Some of the items in the Put Away bag don't belong in such boxes. You have old newspaper clippings, warranties, instruction booklets, receipts for major purchases, and so on. Now it's time to use our file folders. Here are some of the labels you might want to have on your folders:

1—Report cards
2—Appliance instructions
3—Warranties
4—Decorating ideas
5—Insurance papers and booklets
6—Special notes, letters, and cards

7—Car repair receipts
8—Receipts for major purchases
9—Medical

Keeping It Organized

You have your house totally clean. Now how are you going to keep it that way? You certainly never want to sort through all that clutter again! Remember our rule: "Don't put it down, put it away." That alone will save stress. Just discipline yourself to handle an item once and put it directly away. You will be glad to know you won't have to do it again.

Your next task is to take your 3"×5" cards and tabbed dividers. Label the dividers with the following categories:

In the garage, assign labeled "parking spaces" for bicycles, lawnmowers, gardening tools, etc. If someone fails to "park" an item in it's proper place, issue a "ticket" and charge a small fine.

- ⊕ Daily
- ⊕ Weekly
- ⊕ Monthly
- ⊕ Quarterly
- ⊕ Biannually
- ⊕ Annually
- ⊕ Storage

Assign a color of index cards to each section. On the first set of cards, list those jobs you do daily, such as washing the dishes, making the bed, and picking up around the house. On the next set of cards, list your weekly chores, on the next set, your monthly chores, and so on. Below are suggestions for dividing the household tasks.

Daily Chores

- wash dishes
- make beds
- check bathrooms
- pick up rooms
- pick up kitchen

Weekly Chores

- Monday—wash, plan menu
- Tuesday—iron, water plants
- Wednesday—mop floors
- Thursday—vacuum, grocery shop
- Friday—change bed linens, dust
- Saturday—yardwork
- Sunday—free (except plan for next week!)

Monthly Chores

- Week 1—clean refrigerator
- Week 2—clean oven
- Week 3—wax furniture
- Week 4—clean and dust baseboards

Quarterly Chores

- straighten drawers
- clean windows
- clean closets
- move furniture and vacuum
- dust and straighten china cabinets
- clean cupboards
- clean mini-blinds

Biannual Chores

- clean screens
- rearrange furniture

Annual Chores

- wash curtains
- clean carpets
- prune trees
- clean drapes
- clean out garage/basement/attic

Now let's say Thursday comes along and your good friend Sue calls and says, "Let's go to lunch, then do some shopping. The department store has a big sale today." So you check your card file and say, "I've done all my daily things, but it's Thursday, so I have to vacuum and go to the market. I can do my marketing this afternoon when we get back, but I don't know about the vacuuming."

You move vacuuming to Friday, but there's already a list of things to do. So you move your Friday chores to Saturday, but you promised the kids you'd take them to the park. But moving the chores to Sunday isn't going to work either because you have company coming over after church! By Monday morning you have a million things to do, and the house is already starting to look messy again.

So you're not going to move the vacuuming to Friday. Instead, you're going to move it to the back of the weekly section. That's right—you're not going to vacuum again until next Thursday, when the vacuuming card comes up again in the file. Rotate the cards daily, whether you do the allotted jobs or not.

By following this system, you avoid cramming a week's worth of housekeeping chores into one day, and you develop a routine that helps keep your priorities in order. When Sue calls next Thursday and invites you to lunch and shopping, you take one look at your unvacuumed floor and say, "How about I meet you at the mall after lunch? I've got a couple of things I need to finish up around here."

Next you have your monthly chores. During Week 1 you clean the refrigerator. (You have a whole week to do it, or you can delegate the job to one of your children.) During Week 2 you do the oven, and so forth. This way, every week you're doing a little bit to maintain your home. It's only going to take you a little time, but you're continually tidying up your home so you never have to go through that total mess program again. Next you have your quarterly things to do (straighten drawers, etc.). Then you have your semiannual tasks (rearrange furniture, wash curtains, etc.). Finally, there are the annual jobs such as cleaning the basement, attic, garage, etc.

Your last tab, at the very back of your card file, is your storage tab. Your 3" × 5" cards are numbered Box 1, Box 2, Box 3, and your Perfect Boxes are given a corresponding number. If you want to go a step further, you can make two cards for each box—one to be pasted on the box and one to go

Assign convenient permanent locations for small restless items that would otherwise end up on a tabletop or be mislaid: a hook near the door for keys that you always take when you go out— a small dish on the bureau top to collect loose change or earrings; a mug on the desk to hold pens and pencils.

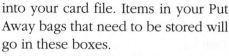

If you can't get all your housework done in a reasonable amount of time, hire someone to help you. You'll be surprised at how much more you can accomplish with someone helping out just three hours every week!

into your card file. Items in your Put Away bags that need to be stored will go in these boxes.

Now you take the file box and the colored file folders and look at what's left in the Put Away bags. What do you find? Old newspaper articles, appliance manuals, receipts, and all kinds of other things. So we put these papers in our colored file folders, label the folders (see the suggested list on pages 77–78), list all those things on 3" × 5" cards, and file the cards away under "Storage" in our file box.

As you begin to develop a business at home, it is vital that your house and your office be consistently clean and tidy. This will allow you the freedom to work at your business and not feel guilty for any cleaning left undone. It will also assure that when clients do come to your office, you have the appearance of a true professional. This plan will work for any area of your home including wardrobe closets and the garage.

Make sure to have your children help out as much as possible with the household chores. They will help you to save time while you will teach them valuable lessons in responsibility and family loyalty. In another chapter we will discuss different chores your children can do at different ages.

So, what have you done using Emilie's method? You've taken a big step toward simply organizing your house—and maintaining that organization. What does that give you? More hours in your day, with no guilty feelings about a cluttered house or office. You can now manage your business with confidence.

If you can't afford professional help, be creative. Possible sources of assistance include schoolchildren, college students, and neighbors who might be willing to take over one or two jobs, such as housecleaning, ironing, or grocery shopping—and for considerably less than it costs to hire a professional.

HOMEwork

If you cannot find time to do what you want, here is how to make time:

1. Delegate some of the household work to other family members.

2. Eliminate some of the work entirely. (You don't have to iron certain items that you do.)

3. Make sure all of your children contribute to running the household.

4. Use small amounts of time (five-to-ten minute blocks) to your best advantage.

5. Carefully plan the use of leisure time. Concentrate on doing those activities that give you real pleasure.

6. Leave yourself some open-ended time for a spur-of-the-moment activity. Do not cram your appointment book full of things to do.

Making Time for Your Husband

This is a critical chapter in helping to determine whether your business or idea for a business can and will succeed. Next to the financial considerations, your husband is generally concerned about how he will fit into your schedule. If you have children, he already takes second place many times because of the natural considerations that must be made for children. Their needs are immediate and simply out of necessity husbands must sometimes take a backseat. For most husbands this is a natural occurrence and they make the necessary adjustments. However, in his eyes, a home-based business may not be a priority over him. I (Emilie) often say, "You were a wife to your husband before you were a mother to your children." In that same vein, I (Sheri) add, "Your husband needs to feel important and part of the business in order to be supportive." He doesn't want to be made to feel that his needs are unimportant. Men depend on their wives in ways we are not even aware. They seem to be so independent in their work and play, but they do have a fundamental need to feel important to their wives. Husbands need respect and a sense that they are a top priority to their wives. There are many ways to make your husband a priority even when you are juggling children, a home, and a business.

My (Emilie's) Bob and I have been married for 43 years. After that much time together, I know what makes him tick and what is important to him. I balance an extremely busy schedule, yet still let him know that he is the most important person in my life when we are together. After I return home from an out-of-town seminar, I spend time setting up a special breakfast or lunch. Sometimes it is outside, sometimes it is inside in our breakfast nook. I love to complete it with flowers and candles. Bob and I spend time together unhurriedly discussing plans and dreams and reconnecting with each other. Over the years we have discov-

Schedule your "dates" in your planner just as you would for a client or customer. Your spouse will feel special.

ered the principle that in order to be happily married, both our needs are vitally important.

I (Sheri) have been married for 21 years to my husband, Tim, and will eagerly tell you that it is very important to me that Tim feels that he is a priority when he is home. Because of his unusual work schedule, on duty 24 hours at a time, I plan time with friends and family, lunch with a friend, or shopping trips on the days he works. I am even able to juggle client appointments and hectic days around the days when Tim is on duty. By working from home, I am also free to schedule an impromptu drive to the beach for lunch or a relaxing day working in our backyard together.

Making time for your husband is not difficult and doesn't have to cost anything other than a little imagination and the desire to find what makes him happy. We have discovered that men really don't need or want a lot of fuss. They prefer very simple demonstrations of love and devotion. Both of us have discovered that when wives make their husbands a priority, the husbands are happy and contented and eager to please.

Many of you reading this book may be thinking, "Oh great, someone else telling me what I'm doing wrong with my husband." On the contrary, it is a wise woman who has discovered that the secret to true happiness in marriage comes when one person decides to make the other person his or her priority and refuses to be selfish. We agree that a loving attitude reaps far greater rewards from our husbands. Just as God wants you to give out of a cheerful heart, we as wives must have that same attitude. Not "I have to," but "I want to."

So where do you begin? Listed below are some tried-and-true examples of ideas that you can use in your own relationship. Please keep in mind that they are merely suggestions. Change and adapt them to fit your own husband and what he likes. Some of you will experience immediate rewards from making your husband the priority he deserves to be. For some of you, it may take a little longer. Don't give up. God honors our efforts and asks that we only be willing.

- Ask your husband's advice on how to place the furniture in your office or work area for the best use of space.

- If he is good at organization, let him give you some pointers on how best to arrange files and paperwork.

- Make him lunch and serve it outside, taking time to admire his beautiful handiwork in the yard.

- Leave a sweet note in the bathroom near his shaving cream and razor.

- If he is a sports nut, prepare finger foods for Monday Night Football and spread out a blanket on the floor. Join him on the floor eating and watching the game.

- Make arrangements ahead of time to send the children to Grandma's or a sitter and spend a quiet evening home alone with a candlelight dinner.

- Thank him for all he does to provide for the family.

- Surprise him and iron several of his shirts ahead of time.

- Make his favorite breakfast and have it ready before he leaves for work.

- Within earshot, praise him to a special friend or neighbor or extended family member.

- Surprise him and mow the yard for him so he can take some time to play golf or take the kids to the park. You can also pay a teenager in the neighborhood to mow it.

- Hire a teenager to wash and clean his car.

- Meet him at work for lunch with a "love basket" and surprise him by going to a park to enjoy each other's company and his favorite food.

- Let him sleep in and serve him breakfast in bed.

- Rent his favorite movie and watch it with him.

- Buy him a new shirt with some of the money you earned from your business.

- Thank him for supporting you in your home-based business.

- Tell him how much you love him at least once every day.

- If you can, call him during the day for no reason except to tell him you are thinking of him and can't wait for him to come home.

- Purchase tickets for a sporting event or ballgame that you know he would love to go to. Go to the game together!

- Remember that confidence and strength are qualities he really admires in a wife.

- Prepare his favorite dinner to celebrate a raise or promotion at work or a milestone in your business.

Just as women need "I love yous" and flowers, men need our respect, strength, and devotion. Without those he will begin to lose confidence in who he is and what his role is in the family. As a wise woman, you can demonstrate that respect in many different ways. Don't be afraid to tackle new areas in your marriage. What you will learn will only serve to strengthen your family as a whole.

HOMEwork

Make sure to set aside a specific day and/or time each week for your spouse. Because you are working at home, it may be lunch out together instead of dinner. Be creative. Don't forget to nurture your relationship.

Family Time Together

O ne of the biggest hurdles you will face once you make the choice to come home and work will be scheduling family time. Although the stresses of working outside the home will be gone, you will have an adjustment time figuring out how to organize your family and work at home. There are many advantages to living and working under the same roof, but there are also disadvantages that must be addressed. Organization is the key to success at almost anything. So much of a family's stress is due to disorganization. Organization is a process, however, that needs to be worked at a little bit at a time rather than having unrealistic expectations that everything will be

Get your family to help out with errands. If a shirt has to be returned, leave it in plain sight so that anyone going to or near the particular store can return it. To make it easy, attach a note with instructions— credit to charge account, exchange for a different size or color, etc.

organized and running smoothly overnight.

For most of you reading this book, your choice to come home most likely was determined by your need to spend more time with your family. You wanted to be there to raise your children instead of placing them in day care or preschool. This is admirable and the decision to come home is not an easy one. Get ready, because now the work begins!

Depending on the ages of your children, your plan for scheduling family time together will differ. When your children are infants and toddlers, you will determine the activities in which you are involved. As they grow older, school activities and friendships begin to chip away at the precious time you have to spend together. As their social circles and activities grow, so does the time they spend away from home.

You may have been told that quality time precludes the need for quantity time. Nothing could be further from the truth. You have possibly heard on television or read in magazines that all you need to raise well-adjusted, delightful children is just a few minutes of undivided attention each day and that will replace hours of at-home time together. This is simply not true. Even while doing the dishes, you are teaching your children. Being available to kiss the boo-boos, clean a scraped knee, or listen to the latest story of school-day adventures can never be replaced by time spent with a day care worker or babysitter. When a child is hurt or crying, no one can replace Mom or Dad. Remember, no one will love your children the way you do. You know how to make them feel better, feel secure, and feel loved.

When I (Sheri) was young, my mother would send the kids outside to play while she cleaned the house. We were only allowed to come in to use the restroom, eat lunch, or help Mom with a chore. It was such a memorable time in my childhood—romping around with the neighborhood kids, swimming in the afternoons, and coming in to help with dinner. It was very comforting to come home from school and know that Mom was home. Most afternoons dinner was already in preparation. I knew that I was loved and important. When my mother had to return to work when I was in junior high school, I was devastated. No more coming home to sweet smells and a listening ear. Even though I had a wonderful nanny, it was never the same.

I (Emilie) worked in my mother's dress shop after my father passed

Set up an emergency shelf out of reach of small children. Equip it with flashlights, candles (use votive candles in glass holders for safety), matches, a first aid kit, and an index card that lists emergency numbers. Make sure the babysitters know where the shelf is located.

If you have appointments or errands at several different locations, schedule them so that you can go from one place to the next with a minimum of wasted time and travel. Eliminate additional trips by making back-to-back doctor or dentist appointments for the whole family (or at least for all the kids).

away. We worked side by side and although we did not have much money, I have many fond memories of the time I spent working with my mother. Much of what I teach today came from lessons I learned in that dress shop many years ago. My mother taught by loving example. She was there for her children and knew the importance of raising them and not leaving it up to someone else.

You must understand that any sacrifices you make to be at home with your children will reap tremendous rewards later in life. You will be amazed at what events and occurrences your children will remember.

Before my (Sheri's) mother returned to work, I remember a day spent with Mom and my siblings that seems just like it happened yesterday. Money was very tight, so Mother packed a very simple lunch of tuna sandwiches, chips, and iced tea. She took us four children to the park nearby to play. There was a donut shop on the way and she purchased five donuts to serve as dessert with lunch. I remember playing for what seemed like hours and hours. Tuna sandwiches and donuts never tasted so good! We returned home late in the evening, exhausted but glowing in the fun we'd had. That trip occurred over 30 years ago and yet the memories are as vivid today as they were then. It doesn't take a lot of money or an exciting venue to make memories. Sometimes the simplest outings provide those treasured moments.

Since many of you working from home will be dealing with limited incomes, it is important to remember that simple and inexpensive is usually better. How many times have your children awakened on Christmas morning and, after tearing into their mountains of gifts, spent more time playing with the boxes the gifts came in rather than the gifts? Keep the focus on making memories, not piling up debt.

Following are some of our favorite ways to ensure that you, your husband, and children spend excellent family time together.

Guidelines and Ideas

Insist that dinner meals be eaten together.

When they are young, teach your children that activities and friends can and will wait until after dinner. Of course there will be exceptions, but try not to make them the rule. This really becomes an issue once your children are teenagers, but if they are taught early on to recognize the importance of the family dinner, they will respect it as well.

My (Emilie's) children are grown and gone and I have five grandchildren. I instilled in my children the importance of the family mealtime and my grown children have continued this great family tradition. In fact, I still prepare special family dinners on Sundays or on evenings when I'm not traveling. It is still important to get together even after the children are grown and have families of their own.

My (Sheri's) two children are teenagers and both have jobs. It is becoming more difficult to have everyone home at the same time for dinner, especially with my husband's unusual schedule. However, when I do know that everyone is going to be home, I prepare a special dinner for the family.

Don't answer the telephone during the dinner hour.

One of the greatest inventions of this century is the answering machine. It allows your family to enjoy uninterrupted time together without missing out on any important messages. Tell your children at a young age that their friends must not call during dinner. Stick to your rules and you won't have a problem as the kids become teenagers.

Turn off the television.

One of the saddest commentaries of this country is our fixation with the television. Insist that during the dinner hour, the TV must be off.

I (Sheri) recall a two-year period when our family did not have a television. Tim and I decided that TV had become the centerpiece of the family and that there really were not many programs worth watching. At first the children whined and complained, but it didn't take long before they became used to life without the television. We spent more time talking to each other, listening to good music, and even playing games together. It provided an excellent opportunity for us to get reconnected.

Activity Ideas

✎ Prepare a tea party for your young children, one child at a time. It helps them feel special and usually brings about some very interesting dialogue. If you start out when they are young, they will cherish the tradition when they are older. Don't forget to have tea parties for boys as well as girls. The decorations and what you serve to eat should be different, but boys enjoy feeling special, too.

↝ Schedule one day each month for each of your children. Allow them to choose what you will do and where you will go, keeping in mind finances and time constraints. Schedule this "date" just as you would a date with your husband or an appointment with a client. You are teaching your children character by respecting what you have promised to do. They learn what you live!

↝ Put each family member's favorite meal on a slip of paper and, when preparing your weekly dinner schedule, pull out a piece of paper and prepare that family member's meal. On the night that person's favorite dinner is served, let him or her help as much as possible—setting the table, folding napkins, stirring sauces, etc. At dinner have the family member tell how this dish became his or her favorite and why he or she likes it so much.

↝ One of my (Sheri's) children's favorite memories is the famous "PJ Ride." After the children were fed, bathed, and dressed for bed, I would creep into their bedrooms right after they were tucked in and yell, "PJ Ride!" I could hear their excited giggles and laughter all down the hall and into the car. I would then take them to the local McDonald's restaurant or to the ice cream parlor where we would enjoy a special treat. The children never knew when a PJ Ride would occur, and if they asked for one it eliminated the chances of having one that evening. It only took an extra hour of my time but the rewards were great.

HOMEwork

Establish a message center in your home. It needn't be elaborate—it can be on the refrigerator or on a bulletin board or door. Encourage everyone in the household to use the message center to list plans, needs for the next trip to the grocery store, and—especially important—all telephone messages. Keep the message center current; throw away outdated notes. Take care of as many items as you can in one day—or enter them in your notebook for action later.

Coming Home to Work

The Miller Family
Brian, Laura, and Baby Mollie

On November 1, 1997, Laura quit her job as an executive secretary for a large retail firm where she had worked for over 10 years and began working at her husband's auto glass business, which he had started earlier that year.

Brian had been working in the auto glass industry for eight years—seven years with a national auto glass company and one year with a small family-owned company. He decided to start his own business because the national company was structured so that advancement was almost impossible, and he was already at the top of the pay scale.

Within a month of working with Brian and getting over her initial "stage fright" of starting a new job, Laura was pleased to note that the business was growing in both volume and income. In fact, the Millers actually turned work away on some days. They were sometimes booked several days in advance, and this really boosted their confidence.

Brian and Laura recently purchased their first home and their precious baby girl, Mollie, was born shortly thereafter. She is the joy of their lives. Laura will now be able to work side-by-side with Brian and contribute to the business *and* be a stay-at-home working mom. The Millers are seeing their dreams come true because of the business.

Laura now realizes that staying at home to work has actually saved the family money. Although she doesn't have the income she had as an executive secretary, she has been able to incorporate her acquired skills into the family business. She spends less time—actually, no time—on the road. She does not spend anywhere near the amount of money on clothes, shoes, and accessories as she did working in a corporate setting. She also spends next to nothing on gas and repairs, and auto maintenance has decreased significantly. Laura cannot even begin to imagine how much wear and tear she is saving on her body and mind now that she is free from the stress of commuting. In fact, she looks back and wonders how she ever spent year after year commuting anywhere from 45–90 minutes each way. She can't begin to imagine how much money the family is saving annually by having her work at home. Just the savings in day care alone are incredible. Best of all, she will be the one seeing her daughter's first steps and hearing her first word. No amount of money could ever compare to that.

It is very rewarding for Laura to stay home and take care of her baby, her husband, and their business. The Millers spend family time together on the weekends. They have discovered that working at home has more benefits than just staying at home. It gives Laura the opportunity to keep up on her business skills and stay abreast of things going on in the workforce. She is also able to communicate with customers and other business associates, responsibilities she enjoyed in her previous job. Brian and Laura have met many people and even made new friends through the business. Laura never imagined all the benefits of working at home. It is a decision she has never regretted.

Chapter
Ten

Dinner's on
the Table

The average woman cooks, plans, markets, and cleans up more than 750 meals a year! Doesn't it stand to reason that this is a major area where there is a need for organization? Feeding the family is certainly a big part of life, so we'd like to share our favorite easy steps and hints to making meal planning and preparation successful. Again, advance planning and organization are the keys.

Keep It Simple

↦ Because you are now living and working under the same roof, it is vital that you devise a plan that is not only simple but created to work with your family. You know your family best so tailor your meal planning to suit their needs.

Keep a running list of groceries and household supplies that you need. By the time you're ready to go shopping, there will be little to add.

⚭ Fold an 8½" × 11" sheet of paper lengthwise in half. Fold that half crosswise and then in half again to equal eight squares. Write the names of the days of the week in seven of the squares and "rest" in the eighth square.

⚭ Select a main dish for each of the seven squares and plan your meals accordingly. In your planning, remember to consider eating out, having company, serving leftovers, and including family favorites. Post your meal planner chart so that all family members can see it. In case you are running late with a client, your husband or older children can check the planner and start dinner for you.

⚭ If you have a computer, you can save time by keeping on it a simple form with the squares and days of the week already there. Just fill in the meals. You can also list on your meal planner which person in the family is responsible for setting and/or clearing the table for that day or week.

Work Your Plan

- Now take your planner and from it make a marketing list. This eliminates buying items you don't need or forgetting a necessary ingredient. You can also create a shopping list on your computer where you simply check off what items are needed that week.

- To save time, list items as they appear in the supermarket aisles. This will prevent you from back-tracking and spending more money. A study showed that after the first half-hour in the market, a woman will spend at least 75 cents per minute! You'll find you will be able to complete your shopping within 30 minutes if you've organized your list and you've determined to stick to it.

- Shop, if possible, at off hours (early morning, late evening). This is a great time to utilize your calendar and to-do list. Schedule your shopping days each month as you would any other appointment. This will also help you to keep the shopping time to a minimum. Shop alone—both your husband and your children can cause you to compromise on

The problem with storage closets and kitchen cabinets is remembering everything that is in them. Taping an overall list to the inside of the door saves you the time and trouble of searching for something that may be in the back of a cabinet or at the bottom of the closet—or may not be there at all!

your list. And never shop when you're hungry because then you'll be tempted to buy junk food and things you really do not need.

⊷ Beware of supermarket psychology. Higher-priced items are stocked at eye level. Food displays at the ends of aisles may appear to be on sale but often are not.

Other Helpful Hints

⊷ If you have a teenage driver in the family, let him or her handle the marketing for you. You are teaching some valuable lessons for later on in life. Preteens and teenagers can also help with the meal planning and preparation. This will free up your time to continue working without feeling stressed.

⊷ Don't forget Tupper Suppers—premade meals that are stored in plastic containers in the freezer or refrigerator. Whenever possible, double a recipe and freeze the other half. This will be a bonus on particularly hectic days, perhaps Mondays or Fridays.

⊷ To speed up baking potatoes, simply put a clean nail through each potato. They will cook in half the time. (Don't try this in the microwave!)

⊷ Leftover pancakes or waffles? Don't discard them; freeze them. Then pop them into the toaster oven for a quick and easy breakfast or after-school snack. There is something fun about having breakfast food at a time other than breakfast. Kids love the change of pace!

⊷ Freeze lunchbox sandwiches. They can be made fresh each week. Put on all ingredients except lettuce and dressings. It will save time and speed up those early mornings.

↝ No need to boil those lasagna noodles for casseroles anymore! Just spread sauce in the bottom of the pan, place hard, uncooked noodles on top, and spread sauce on top of noodles. Continue with the other layers, finishing with noodles and sauce. Cover with foil and bake at 350 degrees for 1 hour and 15 minutes.

↝ Before freezing bagels, cut them in half. When you're ready to use them, they will defrost faster and can even be toasted while they are still frozen.

↝ Make ground beef or turkey into patties before freezing. Freeze four ¼-lb. patties to a package with wax paper in between. If you need a pound of meat for a recipe, use all four patties. They will be ready for hamburgers in just a few minutes for a last-minute dinner. You can barbecue frozen patties, too!

↝ Fruit prepared ahead of time (quartered, in fruit salads) will keep well if you squeeze lemon juice over it and refrigerate it.

Use labor-saving gadgets or appliances whenever they'll really save time. But don't overdo it—chopping an onion with a knife may take no longer than using a food processor and then having to take it apart to wash and dry it.

The juice of half a lemon is enough for up to two quarts of cut fruit.

By spending a little extra time preparing your food and planning your meals, you'll save even more time for the other things you need to do! My (Emilie's) book *Simply Dinner* is an excellent recipe book with some delicious recipes. I also have written several other cookbooks that provide delicious recipes and helpful tips to save time in the kitchen.

Ten Benefits of Meal Planning

1. Saves you time.
2. Saves you money.
3. Eliminates stress.
4. Prevents making bad choices.
5. Gives you better nutrition.
6. Makes happy homes.
7. Makes happy mealtimes.
8. Makes happy children.
9. Makes happy husbands.
10. Makes a very happy mom who has a very happy family!

HOMEwork

If you have preteen or teenage children, get them in the habit of grocery shopping and learning how to shop efficiently. As you shop you are teaching your children many things. Teach them to clip coupons. When your total comes up at the register, write the check for the full amount and then turn in your coupons. Give whatever is saved to your children to put in their college fund or savings account for something special. You will make it worth their while to learn how to shop wisely.

Chapter
Eleven

Working
with the Children

B y now you have probably no doubt realized that one of the greatest challenges to working at home is discovering how to work with children. Remember, your children are the primary reason many of you decided to come home in the first place. We are seeing an increasing trend of mothers returning home after discovering that the super-mom syndrome was a big lie. These same mothers are seeing the worth of raising their children and becoming makers of their homes. And the really exciting part is that men are beginning to see the value of their wives being home to raise the children. As you plan to bring your work home, remember that we are all given the same amount of time each day. What counts is what we do with it.

Keep an empty basket by your children's bedroom doors. When you find toys and articles of clothing scattered around, place them in the respective baskets or delegate this job to one of your children.

As you know, I (Sheri) began my typing and word processing business while pregnant with my first child. I now know firsthand what to expect and understand how it is possible to operate a successful business with children underfoot. One of my greatest discoveries was realizing that my business was growing slowly and naturally right along with my children. When the children were babies, I was not able to accomplish as much typing as I am able to now. I also became very creative in how I managed my work time and my time with the kids. I scheduled appointments around their naps. I worked very early in the morning (fortunately, I am a true morning person) before anyone was awake and also after the children went to bed in the evening. And I learned not to expect too much from the business while the children were infants and toddlers. I understood the importance of my role as mother first and businesswoman second. I've learned a few guidelines to working at home with small children that will help you:

↬ Don't have unrealistic expectations for your business. Let the business grow naturally. Set small, manageable goals and reward yourself when those goals are met.

◆ Schedule appointments around children's schedules.

◆ Handle tasks that can be completed while your kids play or sleep nearby (e.g., writing notes, organizing the next day's activities and appointments in your planner, planning your errands in order of importance, etc.).

◆ Set aside specific times to devote your complete attention to the children. Go to the park or take a walk. The diversion will do you some good as well. When you come back you will be refreshed and ready to conquer the next task.

◆ Don't expect to give one hundred percent to your business while your children are infants and toddlers. You must be willing to divide your time between your children and the business.

◆ Stop occasionally while working just to give your child a hug. It will do you both a world of good.

Put books and games on lower shelves in the playroom, and paint, clay, scissors, crayons, or anything you don't want kids to play with unsupervised on the upper, out-of-reach shelves.

Realize that your primary job will be mothering during the early years before your children start school. It will take an enormous burden off your shoulders regarding expectations for your business. This does not mean that your business cannot succeed or make money, but the focus is on family first and the business second. Remind yourself often that the reason you came home in the first place is to be there for your children. Set realistic goals for what you want your business to accomplish. Be patient with yourself and understand that occasions will arise when the business must take a priority, but let them be the exception rather than the rule.

What are some ways to effectively combine working at home with raising children? Below are some no-fail methods that will give you some options:

1. Let your husband take care of the children when he can to free up time for you to concentrate on business tasks. Use the uninterrupted time to make telephone calls, schedule appointments, and complete projects. Never make business calls with a crying baby or a barking dog in the background.

2. If you are fortunate enough to have a child's grandparent nearby, schedule times for grandparents to take the children to the park or to a museum. This will allow time for you to concentrate on a specific task or project. If possible, schedule this outing for the same time each week. It will help you in your planning process for your business.

3. If you have older children in the family, pay them a small amount to spend time with their younger siblings playing a game or taking a walk. By paying teenagers, you are saying that their time is valuable, too. It also gives them a chance to earn money for "extras."

4. Do you have a friend with children the same age as your children? Swap babysitting with her. Use your

time during the day to handle business, then reciprocate in the evening when you have closed business for the day.

5. Consider bartering childcare services with a friend in exchange for products or services your home business offers. For example, if you sell cosmetics, offer a free makeover and make-up in exchange for a few hours of babysitting.

You can operate a successful business without sacrificing time with your children if you are organized and spend adequate time planning. As your children grow older, they will become accustomed to seeing you at home in your office. You can begin teaching them at a very young age some valuable tools for working, and they can even begin helping you in your work. My (Sheri's) daughter is quite an accomplished typist. I allow Terra to handle some of my smaller typing projects. At the very least, when Terra starts college she will be able to type all her own papers instead of paying someone to do them for her. She has earned money and a great deal of experience working with her mom. She can also answer the telephone and give price quotes.

Select one shelf in the den or playroom for storing borrowed library books. You'll know where they are when it's time to return them.

I like to tell a fun story about the time when a new client called late in the afternoon while I was out of the office running errands. Terra was 12 years old at the time and answered the business line when it rang. She had been given clear instructions on what to say and what to ask. The client asked some questions about prices for a school paper she needed typed. Terra quoted the price and asked if the client wanted to schedule an appointment. At this point the client was so intrigued by the maturity of the youthful girl on the phone that she decided to make an appointment just to meet the young lady who helped her with such efficiency. When I returned home, Terra proudly told me that a customer would be arriving at 3:00 p.m. the next afternoon. She had placed the client's name and telephone number in the appointment log just as she had been taught. When "Jane" arrived the next afternoon, she couldn't remark enough about how impressed she was with Terra's ability to handle the call with such maturity and efficiency. Jane became a regular client and a special friend as well.

When we teach our children about the business and how it operates, we are giving them tools they will be able to use later in life. Obviously, this is a process that cannot be done overnight. However, the benefits are great and well worth the effort.

So how do you include your children in the business and let them feel like a part of it rather than a distraction? Delegating responsibility to children is such an important aspect of motherhood that you should be giving your children things to do at a very young age. We are instructed in the Bible to train our children in the right direction. We are then given the promise that when they grow up they will not move away from what they learned as small children.

One of the most overwhelming parts of working at home is accomplishing our daily household chores quickly and efficiently in order to have time to spend growing a successful business. One of the best ways to do this is to teach children early on how to complete tasks and to let them handle age-appropriate chores. It is never too early to begin to teach our children responsibility. Before they are old enough to handle actual chores for themselves, they will learn from watching you. You can begin to teach them simple chores when they're as young as two and three years old. You will lessen your stress level and that overwhelming feeling of frustration that you can't get everything done. At the same time, you will be teaching your children lessons for life.

My (Emilie's) children are grown with families of their own, but by the time they were teenagers they knew how to clean a home, wash their laundry, and cook meals. I thoroughly prepared them to be productive adults. My (Sheri's) children are now older teenagers and they, too, can cook, clean, and do the wash. Nick is preparing to go to college in a few months, and I am confident that I have given him the tools to enable him to take care of himself. Terra can completely prepare and serve a full Thanksgiving dinner. This not only makes me proud, it also reassures me

Use drawstring pouches made from fabric as containers for baby blocks, puzzle pieces, and other toys with dozens of parts.

that I can let my children move into adulthood confident that they will be self-sufficient young adults.

We by ourselves cannot do it all in our homes (when we try, we become frustrated), so when we begin to delegate responsibilities to our children, they begin to feel as if they are a vital part of the family. When families work together and play together, they will also love together and pray together. Then we'll raise children who are balanced people, children who become creative adults with wonderful homes of their own.

So what can be expected of your children and at what ages? Here are some guidelines by age that will give you a good start. All children are different and learn and develop at different ages, so please remember that this is only a guide.

Jobs for Your Children

Three-year-old

1. Get dressed, put pajamas away.
2. Brush hair.
3. Brush teeth.
4. Make bed (yes, it will be sloppy, but it gets better in time with practice).
5. Fold clothes and small items.
6. Empty dishwasher (will need help with this).
7. Clear meal dishes.
8. Empty wastebaskets.
9. Pick up toys before bed.

Five-year-old

1. Set table.
2. Clean bathroom sink.

3. Help clean and straighten drawers and closets.
4. Clean up after pet.
5. Feed pet.
6. Walk dog.
7. Dust furniture in room.
8. Vacuum room.
9. Help put groceries away.

Seven-year-old

1. Empty garbage.
2. Sweep walks.
3. Help clean up kitchen after dinner.
4. Help make lunch for school.
5. Do schoolwork.
6. Clean out car.
7. Take piano lessons, etc.
8. Iron flat items.

Eight-year-old

1. Wash bathroom mirrors.
2. Wash windows.
3. Wash floors in small area.
4. Polish shoes.

As your children grow, more responsibilities can be given to them:

1. Wash car.
2. Mow lawn.
3. Make dessert.
4. Paint.
5. Clean refrigerator.

*U*se a zippered mesh lingerie bag for storing bath toys. Tie with string and hang it over the showerhead so toys can drip dry.

6. Do yardwork.
7. Iron.
8. Fix an entire meal.
9. Do grocery shopping.

Children need to know that they are valuable to the family and that they are needed in order for the family and the home business to function properly. It is easier for them to have a positive attitude when they are around people who believe in their worth. Children want to help and feel needed, and they want to do important jobs. The outcome of the job is not as important as helping a child develop skills and capabilities.

We as parents need to take time to train our children. Whenever we appreciate their contributions, no matter how small, we are helping them to see themselves as capable people.

Thank God for the special blessing of your children. Realize that all too soon they will be grown and your job of raising them will be done. Cherish your time together.

HOMEwork

Assign jobs and responsibilities within the family. Children age two to four can put dirty clothes in the hamper or match socks, ages four to seven can dress themselves and clear the table, while those over eight can put away toys and do many chores reasonably well.

Chapter
Twelve

Room for
Your Office

After you have made the decision to work at home, you may be wondering, "Where in the world am I going to put my office?" If your home has little or no extra space, it will really take some creativity to determine where you might put your office. Before you decide on a location, answer the following questions:

1. How much time will you spend working in the home office?

2. Are distractions at a minimum? Can you close off the room completely?

3. Is there adequate lighting? Can lighting be added economically?

4. Do you have an existing phone line(s)?

5. Does the room have enough electrical outlets?

6. Is the room or area comfortable year round (temperature, light, etc.)?

7. Is there room for everything you need?

8. Will you have adequate storage space?

9. Will customers come to your home?

When my (Sheri's) family moved to our current home, one of the main considerations was a place for my office. Next to the home's location, the office was most critical to me. When we first walked through the house, I immediately envisioned my office in the extra room right off the front door and entryway. I was aware of what would be necessary to accommodate my equipment and furniture. I also liked that my clients would be able to enter the office without having to walk through the rest of the house. This was important for optimal professionalism and a good first impression! After some minor construction changes and decorative touches, my "spare room" was transformed.

Bob and I (Emilie) added the necessary space to our home to accommodate our fast-growing and expanding More Hours In My Day business. We are very careful that any changes enhance our delightful home. I love to do creative designing and decorating, and it's important that the rooms in our house reflect our tastes and personalities.

Keep in mind that if you eventually plan to sell your home, removing a closet in a spare bedroom no longer allows the room to be considered a bedroom. Make additions and transformations that can easily be changed back to original design.

Consider some of the following ideas for home office locations. Try not to eliminate areas simply because they currently do not function as office space. It is amazing what transformations in furniture, paint, and decor can do to change the look of a room. As well, don't assume that you must have an entire room for an office. Don't think of it the way it is now. Think of what it can *become*. Be creative and use your imagination!

- A spare bedroom or family room.
- A dining room that is not used for dining.
- A small section of a room that is not in a high-traffic area.
- An attic or basement.
- A room over a garage.
- A living room (if you also have a family room).
- A section of the garage that can be enclosed.

Get rid of extra paper. Almost 90% of the paper in your home or office is never looked at again. Get rid of as much of it as possible.

Could you possibly move two children into one room to free up a bedroom? You will want to make major changes only if everyone involved is in agreement, but many times two brothers or two sisters might like the change and a chance to room together.

Once a room or area has been chosen, it is wise to sketch out how to

Having more than one phone can be a frustration as well as a convenience. Keep a list of frequently called numbers beside each of the phones. Emergency numbers and numbers of close relatives are a must. In a stressful situation, you may forget.

place the furniture and equipment in order to use the space most effectively. This saves you time and energy and prevents you from moving desks and chairs over and over again trying to find the best layout. When planning your layout, consider the following:

- If your customers or clients come to your home office, place your desk facing the entry so your back will not be to your clients.

- If you have a window in the room, avoid placing your computer monitor so it faces that window. The glare will cause eye strain, especially if you will be spending many hours a day at your computer.

The layout in your office or work area needs to be arranged in such a way that you are not spending too much time moving from one area to another. Set equipment that you will use frequently closest to you. If you receive many telephone calls, don't place the phone out of reach. You'll waste too much time getting up and down to answer the phone. Consider a portable telephone that you can keep on your desk to save time.

Office Organization:
Getting Control of the Clutter

If you are just starting out, you can organize your office right away to make the best use of your time and energy. However, if you already have an office area set up, you may need to go back and rearrange things to make the best use of your business area.

When your office is too cluttered, you cannot utilize your time wisely. You spend more time trying to find things than you should. Clutter gets to you in two ways—physically and, more importantly, psychologically. How many times have you thrown up your hands in despair because of the clutter and mess in your office? Many of us have been there. We feel defeated before we even begin.

By adding some cabinets, shelving, or closet organizers, you can eliminate a great deal of your office clutter.

A Clean Desk...

The Wall Street Journal published a survey recently where 52 business executives were asked the following question: Would you promote someone with a clean desk rather than someone with a cluttered and messy desk? Fifty-one out of 52 executives said they would promote someone who kept a clean desk. Surprised? You shouldn't be. Being neat, however, doesn't always mean that you are organized. Organization can be defined quite simply as the ability to find what you want, when you want it. Or, "It's not where do I put it, but where do I find it?" There is a big difference. How many times have you tried to retrieve a particular piece of paper (even on a clean desk!) only to find that you have absolutely no idea where you put it?

A clean desk gives the impression of a person who is organized and hardworking. Depending on the type of business you operate, a clean desk gives the impression of quality. What clutters up an office and a work area quicker than anything else? Paper clutter. Paper clutter can be found everywhere—at home and in the office. When you combine living and working under the same roof, you can wind up with twice as much paper clutter. Here are some quick tips to keep the mess at a minimum.

- ꙮ My (Emilie's) motto is: "Don't put it down, put it away." Handle paper only one time if at all possible.

- ꙮ Open incoming mail over your trashcan or recycling bin. You can immediately get rid of the junk. Also, get rid of all envelopes. (You'll see a 50% reduction in paper clutter immediately.)

- ꙮ Have a tickler filing system set up and use it. Place each piece of paper into a file immediately after receiving it. Customize your system to fit your personality. If it is too difficult, you'll never use it.

- ꙮ Once you have set up working files, remember they need to be purged regularly.

- ꙮ Tear out articles from magazines that you can read later. Place them in your "5-Minute File." When you've read the article, either file it for later reference or THROW IT AWAY!

- ꙮ Check with your accountant or CPA to determine how long you need to keep old business records. As soon as you can, get rid of them and don't look back.

✧ Throw away warranty books and boxes as soon as the warranty expires. Equipment and supply boxes take up enormous amounts of space.

✧ Donate magazines to your doctor or dentist. Don't save magazines longer than a year. If you haven't read them in a year, you probably never will.

Use the last 15–20 minutes of your workday to clear your desk and eliminate clutter. There is nothing more psychologically defeating than starting your day at a messy desk. A fresh desk that is free of clutter helps your day get off to a good start. So what does your desk reveal about you and how much work you can accomplish? Take a long, hard look and begin to get rid of clutter.

Organize your files

The old cliché "less is better" really applies to your desk. As we stated earlier, you'd be more likely to get a promotion with a clean desk, so don't put too much on it. Avoid cluttering your desk with unnecessary supplies that can be stored just fine in a drawer. Keep cute personal items such as pictures, plants, and souvenirs to a minimum. One box of Kleenex is all your desk needs.

Working papers and files are other major contributors to desk clutter. You can keep them close at hand without having them all over your desk. An organization system for your files is the answer. Every person is different and it is important that you find and use a system suited to your personality. It doesn't matter how exciting a program sounds if you don't use it. There are many books and tapes available that promote organization tools and systems. Find one that suits you and begin to incorporate it into your business. Take it one step at a time:

1. Get a system and stick with it.

2. Set goals for organization and break down the jobs into manageable tasks.

3. Find a planner that will work for you and your particular business and then use it!

What is clutter costing you? Most likely time, money, and customers! You might be extremely intelligent and talented; however, if you are unorganized every step you take will be a struggle. You will find yourself working twice as hard as other people simply because you never learned the basic principles of organization.

In our fast-paced, technological business world, efficiency is more important than ever before. And being organized is *not* a personality trait. It is a skill that anybody can learn. It only takes desire and the willingness to apply some basic principles. The secret to running a smooth office is getting organized and maintaining that level of organization. Once you've accomplished that, you'll be ready to meet the challenges of each new day with a clean office and renewed energy.

HOMEwork

If you're faced with an overcrowded office—or an overcrowded space where you'd like to put your office—schedule an hour to work on it.

Write it on your weekly list as a project. But don't try to finish the office in one session. When the hour is up, quit. Schedule another hour and then another until the office is done.

Chapter
Thirteen

The Calendar

Have you ever missed an important meeting with a client or a birthday party for one of your children's friends? How many times have you come across an invitation three days after the event? By effectively utilizing a calendar, you can eliminate missed appointments, meetings, and events. If you apply some simple principles and ideas, you will be amazed at how much time can be saved when you use a calendar. A calendar provides essential information that can easily be seen and utilized by all members of the family (at least by those who can read!). Good use of a calendar can mean the difference between being organized and knowing what is going on in the family or dealing with the stress of missed deadlines and appointments. Never again will you have to run around at the last minute buying a gift, finding a sitter, or rescheduling appointments. Calendaring takes discipline, especially in the beginning, but the time you invest will increase your productivity and professionalism at home and in your business. As we have discussed in earlier chapters, disorganization causes much of our stress. A well-organized calendar can minimize many of those stresses.

It is important that you use only one calendar for your home and your home business. The reason is simple. If you have too many calendars, the chance of missing an appointment increases. The only exception to this rule is a small daily appointment book for those of you who see clients in your home. You will still need to write in the appointments from the large calendar that fit into your daily schedule.

Make sure the calendar is near the telephone in your home office. Have plenty of supplies on hand near the calendar, including pencils, Post-it notes, and highlight markers. Having the calendar near the office telephone will enable you to immediately check availability while on the phone with a prospective client, a family member,

Set up an area for yourself where you keep all your lists, calendars, menus, etc. This is your place to work and make your calendar schedule.

or a friend. You will be able to make family and business appointments at the same place. It is much easier to make doctor and dentist appointments if you can glance at the calendar while you are on the phone with the doctor's office. You appear much more efficient and organized if you don't need to put someone on hold to search for the calendar or something to write with.

By spending just an hour or so one evening each month, you can prepare your calendar to function as what it was created to be—a self-management tool. This can also be a great time for your family to evaluate your schedules, see what you are spending your time doing, and make any necessary adjustments. It will take practice to make this a routine, but it is not difficult.

Remember to check your calendar each evening before bedtime. That way, you'll already be thinking about your schedule for the next day and what needs to be done first thing in the morning. Also make a simple to-do list the night before and leave it on your desk. You will start your day feeling much more organized if you already have a plan of action for first thing in the morning. We live very hectic and busy lives, especially if we have children and at-home businesses.

If you conduct a lot of business by mail—like paying bills, sending for free offers, or ordering merchandise— enter each transaction on your large wall calendar and check it periodically. This is especially helpful to verify a payment that may have gotten lost or if too much time has elapsed since placing an order.

Your calendar will be a time- and energy-saver that will benefit the whole family.

What You Need

↬ One calendar (at least 11"×17") with large squares (2"×3" minimum) for each day. The squares need to be large enough so you can write several entries in them.

↬ Post-it notes—several different colors and sizes. (Next to the invention of the telephone, I think Post-it notes come in a close second.)

↬ Highlight markers—one color for each family member.

Your calendar can be purchased at an office supply store. They have the best variety of sizes and types, but make sure you get a calendar large enough to be seen from a distance with plenty of writing space.

What You Do

After you have purchased your calendar, markers, and Post-it notes, it's time to begin.

↬ Keep your calendar supplies in a small box or crate so that when you need to work on the calendar you don't spend time looking for the necessary tools.

↬ Pick an evening several days before the end of the month to work on next month's calendar. Turn on the answering machine and turn off the television. Put on a nice CD of instrumental music that creates a relaxed atmosphere.

↬ Keep dinner simple and quick. Once the dishes are done, you're ready to begin calendaring. If you have small children or babies, you might wait to begin until they've been put to bed. If your children are elementary school age, you could have them do their homework nearby.

↬ Begin to mark the calendar in order of importance. First record all the dates that are not flexible, such as work schedules and doctor or dentist appointments.

↬ If you have teenagers, you will need to get information and dates from them regarding their school activities, work schedules, sports activities, etc. Make sure you include these dates on the calendar. This will help you to avoid conflicting with an important date for your business or family.

↬ Color code the month after you have filled it in. In case you forget something or need to make a change, your corrections will be simple and you won't create a messy calendar that is difficult to read. Let your children choose their favorite color. They will get excited when they see "their" color on the calendar—even before they can read. You can also include a color that represents the entire family. Some outings and events will include everyone.

Tips for Success

↬ Record everything on the calendar in pencil just in case a change needs to be made.

↬ As soon as you have scheduled your family vacation time, pencil it in immediately. As the year progresses and other dates come up, you will be sure not to schedule any activities and/or appointments during that time. It is also a cheery visual reminder that vacation time is just around the corner.

✎ Remember to schedule your calendar night each month as well.

✎ When receiving invitations for weddings or showers, put the information on a Post-it note and attach to the month in which the event will take place. Don't pencil it in until you have filled in that particular month's dates. If an RSVP is required, write that information on a Post-it note along with the telephone number and place it on the last day you can RSVP. Once you have called in your RSVP, just pull the Post-it note off and throw it away. You will appear very organized and your host or hostess will be grateful that you remembered to call.

✎ Don't forget to pencil in the "dates" you schedule with your spouse. This is the best way to keep from neglecting that special time together. It also helps to make your spouse feel important.

✎ Schedule playtimes and trips to the park or museum with your children as you would any other appointment. This helps your children to see that they are as important to you as your customers and your business. More important, in fact!

✎ Keep an index card file or small box near the calendar to place invitations in until after the event. The invitation sometimes provides pertinent information that is not necessary to put on the calendar but might be needed later, such as directions to an event or the store where a bride and groom are registered. Keep only current invitations in the box.

By scheduling appointments as far ahead of time as possible, you have a better chance of eliminating scheduling conflicts. If you do run into a conflict, you will have some time to find an alternative date or do some rescheduling. Procrastinating will only get you into trouble. It is much easier to reschedule an appointment three-to-four weeks ahead of time instead of just several days.

I (Sheri) use a very large wall calendar that I place right by my office telephone. Both my residence and business lines are on one telephone, which makes scheduling appointments very easy.

I (Emilie) use a small 8½" × 11" calendar that moves from my office to the front office, or to Bob's office. We color code in a way that is very effective and at a glance can see if we have any available dates to schedule a seminar. We schedule "dates" with each other and protect that time together. We also schedule family outings as well on our calendar even though our children are grown. Time with our children and grandchildren is very important to us.

When you begin using a calendar you may find it a little awkward at first, especially if this is the first time you've tried using a calendar in this manner.

In budgeting time on your daily calendar, leave a cushion of 15 minutes here and there on your schedule. This way you don't find yourself running from one appointment to another.

No matter what kind of work you do from home, effective use of a calendar will make your household run more efficiently, and you will give an impression of professionalism to your at-home business.

HOMEwork

Whenever you receive an invitation to something, attach it to your large wall calendar in the month the event will take place. Also write the event on the calendar on the appropriate day. Keep the invitations clipped to the calendar in one stack and in chronological order. After each event has taken place, remove the invitation. Keeping the invitation handy saves you from searching for the time, the place, and especially the spelling of names.

Chapter
Fourteen

The 5-Minute File

D o you ever find yourself standing in line at the bank, sitting at the car wash, or waiting for a child to come out of school and wish you had something to do during those minutes of waiting? Well, we've been there and we've discovered a solution. The 5-Minute File can be the answer to helping fill up those waiting minutes by focusing on the small tasks that you never seem to have time to do at home.

Recently I (Sheri) decided to try and estimate how many minutes the average person wasted each day. I came up with approximately 2½ hours—in just one day! Now if we had 2½ hours free all in a single block of time, we could

Rarely do we have several free hours to clean out a closet. The key is to use the 5-minute segments you do have to accomplish a small task or make a dent in a larger one. For example, file your nails, make an appointment to see the dentist, or clean just one shelf of that closet. You'll double your efforts if you do small tasks, such as writing a thank-you note, while engaged in some other activity like running a bath or waiting for a casserole to heat. Try talking into a small tape recorder to give yourself reminders while putting on your makeup or taking the bus.

accomplish a great deal. But in 5- or 10-minute segments, not much can get done. Or can it? Think of some small jobs that can be accomplished in very limited amounts of time. For example, did you realize that it only takes three minutes to clean and sanitize a toilet? It will surprise you to discover the short amount of time it takes to do many jobs that you figured would take much longer.

I (Emilie) have always been in favor of utilizing those spare minutes in a useful way. In several of my books, I advocate bringing along an article from a magazine or a book to read while running errands. You never know when you will have a few minutes of waiting.

By now you have realized that time is a premium commodity. I (Emilie) have had women tell me over and over how much they appreciate even an extra few minutes. Juggling a husband, children, a home, and a home business can test even the most organized.

Tasks that can be incorporated into the 5-Minute File will free up time for other important tasks. So what exactly is a 5-Minute File? It's really quite simple. Both of us utilize this concept to eliminate small

142

tasks that can easily become overwhelming. By setting a timer and seeing what you can do in five minutes, you will be surprised by the number of small, tedious jobs you can complete.

What You Will Need

- ⊷ Two sturdy pocket-type file folders (these work best because they keep small papers and notes from falling out).

- ⊷ Stenographer's pad or a computer-generated form.

- ⊷ A timer (preferably one that allows you to set more than one time allotment at the same time. West Bend makes a great timer.

What You Do

- ⊷ Sit down with a cup of tea or coffee (I [Emilie] prefer tea, I [Sheri] love coffee—decaf, of course) and begin making a list of chores and small tasks that can be completed in five minutes or less. Every woman's list will differ, but the concept is the same.

- ⊷ Make a simple chart on your computer or your pad of paper. Include space to check off tasks that you have completed. Some of the items, such as cleaning the toilet or washing out the kitchen trashcan, will be ongoing. However, one-time tasks can be eliminated after they are completed.

- ⊷ You will add and delete items to and from your list regularly, so keep the folder handy.

- ⊷ In one of the file folders, store articles and mail to be read. You can grab it on your way out the door. In the

*Five minute
pickup:
Pick up and dust
in each room
for five minutes.
Time yourself
with a
kitchen timer.*

other folder, keep your computer-generated list. We both suggest making the folder very bright so it's easy to spot for quick retrieval.

So when do you use the 5-Minute File at home? Any time you have a few spare minutes, perhaps when you're waiting for a customer or an important phone call. You might have a few minutes before you leave to pick up a child from soccer practice and don't have time to start a big project.

We've given you sample tasks you can write on your list on pages 145–146. Remember, these are just examples. Be creative and imaginative and have fun! Start with the room closest to your office and work toward the back of the house. You will save time and also clean first the areas that a potential customer might see.

I (Emilie) would like to share one of my favorite timesaving hints: Place all your cleaning products, tools, and utensils in one plastic carryall or large bucket and take it from room to room. This way you won't be looking in different cabinets in different rooms for the window cleaner or furniture polish. Everything will be in one place. Just pick up your carryall and take it with you as you move throughout the house. You will save time, and you'll also save money by not buying more than one of a particular cleaning item. Now here's our list:

- ⊷ Clean the toilet in the guest bathroom.

- ⊷ Shake the floor rug and sweep.

- ⊷ Empty the trashcans. (Timesaving tip: Place a roll of trashcan liners in the bottom of each trashcan. You can remove the trash and put in a new liner immediately.)

- ⊷ Spray and wipe down bathroom mirror(s).

- ⊷ Wipe down outside glass shower door with window cleaner.

- ⊷ Gather dirty bath towels and start a load of laundry.

- ⊷ Fold a load of laundry from the dryer. (Save time by having a color-coded basket for each family member. You save time sorting laundry by folding and placing clothing into individual baskets and placing in the designated rooms.)

- ⊷ Sweep the front walkway. Your customers will notice and it makes a great impression on those new clients.

Break down overwhelming tasks into small jobs; try to limit them to five minutes. Nothing is particularly hard if you divide it up into small segments.

Never have time to read all the magazine articles you'd like to read? When you receive a magazine, quickly go through it and tear out the articles you find interesting. File them away in your 5-minute file for later reading.

✤ Pick some flowers from your garden and arrange them in a vase.

✤ Unload the dishwasher.

✤ Order items over the telephone or on the computer.

✤ Write a thank-you note.

✤ Go through the mail, filing in appropriate family members' color-coded folders. Place items to read later in your 5-Minute File.

✤ Feed and water the animals.

✤ Wipe down computer and printer.

✤ Sharpen all your pencils.

✤ Refill business card holder.

✤ Refill paper in printer.

✤ Work on your to-do list for the next day.

✤ Telephone to confirm any meetings for the next day.

Remember, your children can utilize the 5-Minute File too! Next time they have a few spare minutes waiting for a ride, just hand them the file and let them choose a task that they can complete in five minutes or less. They will be contributing to the family as a whole and utilizing their time responsibly. The main reason we don't get more accomplished is because we lack an organized way to determine what needs to be done. By writing down projects and keeping them in a simple file, you will automatically be organizing yourself and your family.

There is nothing more rewarding than getting tasks completed in a timely manner.

Take your planner with you whenever you go out on errands. You may be able to fit in something that you scheduled for later in the week.

HOMEwork

Many household chores can be done during "in-between" times—in between outings, appointments, or TV programs. Once you realize that it takes only a few minutes to change the sheets, you can fit this and similar tasks into the available time slots.

Chapter
Fifteen

Computers and
Other Equipment

So much has happened in the world of technology since Accu-Pro Typing Service was born in 1979. With nothing more than a desk, one file cabinet, a telephone, and an IBM electronic typewriter, work began. The personal computer was very expensive back then and not readily available for home business.

The concept of working at home started to gain in popularity and those in the field of technology quickly caught on that this was a trend and that a tremendous amount of money could be made in this market. Today hundreds of thousands of people are joining the ranks of the self-employed and those in technology are working hard to provide state-of-the-art equipment that makes working at home faster and easier.

So do you really need a computer? Of course the answer is yes! But that's the easy part. How do you begin to know what you need, where to buy it, and what to ask for?

Some areas you need to think about include:

- ↬ Price
- ↬ Reliability
- ↬ Technical support availability
- ↬ Compatibility with programs and other systems

Beware of advertised computer prices that sound too good to be true. They probably are! You need to read the fine print. For instance, some discount prices don't include a monitor. Some "deals" require that you purchase after-market products to receive the discount price, such as technical support packages. In many cases the discount price is offered after rebates that the consumer is responsible to send in for and claim. Remember, comparable products will have comparable prices. The following questions will serve as guidelines while you search for the best computer to serve the needs of your business.

- ↬ What advantages does this particular computer have over the competition? In other words, why is it a better deal?

- ↬ What types of packages are offered that will combine the best price/performance ratio? For example, if you can purchase a hard drive that has two times more space for $20 more or a hard drive that has four times more space for $60 more, which is the better deal? The smaller hard drive is the better deal in this case. You get more space for less money. Computer prices change *daily* so be careful if you are tempted to buy the newest technology. It is far smarter to buy just below the newest product or upgrade. Not only will you save money, but any "bugs" in the hardware and software will have been worked out.

↬ Is the computer you are interested in upgradeable in any way? How so?

↬ What type of warranty comes with the product? Is this a manufacturer's warranty? Does the company or store offer its own extended warranty? If so, how much does the warranty cost and how long does the coverage last? Is labor included in the extended warranty?

↬ What type(s) of software packages come with the computer system? Does the store offer a discount price on software if the computer is purchased at the same location?

↬ If you have any problems or questions about the product, what options are available?

↬ Does the store or supplier offer additional discounts on multiple computer system orders? Many small, independent retailers do offer discounts so it pays to shop around. It might be worth buying a computer with a friend to get the best price available.

↬ When talking with a sales representative, be sure to explain the purpose and main uses your computer will serve in your business. For example, will your computer need to be networked? Will you need any special input devices to enhance or optimize your work efficiency, such as speech-to-text software, etc.?

These are basic questions that any reputable computer retailer can answer. Don't be afraid to ask other questions

The busy person's greatest need is for "effective," not "efficient," planning. Being effective means choosing the right task from all the alternatives. Being efficient means doing any job that happens to be around. Planning is important because it saves you time in the end. Know what you have to do and have your priorities established.

about areas in which you are unfamiliar. Buying a computer today is easier than it's ever been. It is not the investment it was just a few short years ago, and systems are easier to understand.

What About a Printer?

When deciding what printer is best for you, consider the following questions:

- Will you be printing documents that are required to be "camera-ready"?

- Will you be providing a customer with a final draft of a document for presentation?

- Is most of your computer work done in-house, for your eyes only?

- Do you need to be able to print color documents?

By answering these simple questions, you will be able to decide whether the expense of a laser or color printer is justified or not. If your business requires camera-ready or presentation-quality materials, you will need to invest in a laser printer. Fortunately, laser printers are getting cheaper and cheaper. What cost $3,000 in 1985 now sells for only several hundred dollars. If you need the ability to print in color, you should consider a color ink-jet printer. Hewlett-Packard offers several models and price ranges to fit your budget.[8]

What Other Office Equipment Do I Need?

This is a question that really only you will be able to answer. Try to discern the difference between *needs* and *wants*. Certain types of businesses require certain equipment. Make sure you buy only what you absolutely must have to begin working. Add other equipment as business demands and finances allow.

Furniture

Obviously you will need some office furniture, perhaps a desk and chair, file cabinets, etc. Before you buy anything, look around your home. You may have an old desk stored in the attic or basement collecting dust that would work perfectly. Other places to go for suitable office furniture are garage sales, yard sales, and estate sales. Many times you can get a great deal and a lovely piece of furniture that will enhance your office. Check with family members who may have an old piece of furniture that you can use in a new way in your office. Lisa, a home-based word processor, was given an antique hutch by a family member. The piece was lovely but didn't really fit in with her home decorating style. She innovatively placed the hutch in her office opposite the desk and now uses it as a bookshelf. She also stores supplies in the drawers. It gives her office an elegant look and didn't cost her a penny. Ask friends, family, and neighbors if they have any old pieces of furniture that they are willing to loan out or give away.

If you will be spending a great deal of time at your desk, do invest in a good chair, one that gives back support. You will be able to work for longer stretches of time if the chair is well-made and designed for office work.

Many furniture stores now offer pieces designed especially for the home office. Some even offer free office design services.

Telephones

One basic piece of office equipment that virtually everyone needs is a telephone. The type of telephone you need will vary depending on the type of business you operate. If you place or receive only occasional calls, a standard telephone will work fine. But if you rely on your telephone extensively, as salespeople or consultants do, you may want to invest in some additional features. If you will be working at your computer for a good part of your day, a cordless phone is essential. We recommend purchasing a two-line cordless phone so you don't have to run back and forth between the family telephone and the business telephone. You will save many hours and a lot of frustration. Consider purchasing a headset if you often record information or take

Install telephone jacks all around the house or get a cordless phone so that you can talk wherever you are in and around your home.

notes while on the telephone. It will make you considerably more productive. Make sure the headset is lightweight and designed to last.

If you spend a good deal of time on the road in your car, consider purchasing a cellular phone. Besides allowing you to receive important phone calls, it will enable you to keep in contact with your family as well. Your children will be able to reach you immediately if the need arises. Be careful, however, of the expense. Utilize the cellphone for business purposes so that the charges can be written off as legitimate business expenses. Many companies now offer free weekend minutes. Be sure to check out several different companies, then go with the plan that best suits your needs and finances.

Answering Machines

Several important things to consider when buying an answering machine are quality of the outgoing message, clarity of incoming calls, and reliability and overall quality of the unit. Be aware of these key features:

↝ **Call-screening** allows you to screen calls as they come in without the caller knowing you are listening.

To save time— and frustration— whenever possible use the telephone instead of making a trip. Phone to confirm appointments, to see if a store has the item you want, to learn business hours, etc.

↪ **Voice-activation (VOX)** allows incoming callers to speak for an unlimited amount of time. This is an important feature for business calls where more information needs to be left than just a name and number. Most VOX machines have a device that will automatically cut off after six seconds of silence.

↪ **Two-way recording** allows you to tape a telephone conversation. Machines with this feature will have a beep inserted on the line every fifteen seconds (FCC regulations) to let the caller know that the conversation is being taped.

↪ **Last-message alert** lets you know when the last new message began and ended. This allows you to save messages you wish to keep without listening to them every time you check for new messages.

↪ **Date and time stamp** allows you to play back messages and record the date and time they were received.

Pagers

Pagers are both a blessing and a curse. A pager enables you to contact other pager users at any time. As well, you can be contacted any time. Research the different models and price ranges. Find what is best for you both in service and price.

Fax Machines

The fax machine is one of the most exciting technological developments of this century. A fax is necessary for anyone who needs to share pages of text or copies of documents immediately. Information is transmitted in the time it takes to make a phone call—at the cost of that same phone call. There are many fax machine models from which to choose. Purchase only the features that are necessary to your business. If you will be receiving faxes for information-only reading, don't spend the extra money on a plain-paper fax. It is very costly and unnecessary unless the documents you send are of a legal or permanent nature. An excellent feature that we highly recommend is the paper-cutting feature, which automatically cuts each sheet. It's a great time-saver.

Photocopiers

Most home-based businesses will not have enough need for a copier to warrant the initial purchase of one. This is one of those investments that might come several months or years down the road. Unless your business is doing a high volume of copies on a weekly basis, the cost will be too prohibitive. If you *are* ready to purchase a copier, do thorough research and comparison-shopping before you buy. Purchase one with only the features you need. If you discover that you have a genuine need for a fax and a copier, you can purchase a fax, copier, and printer all in one unit. This might save you more money than if you were to purchase the three machines separately.

Typewriter

Very few businesses today require the use of a typewriter. However, any secretarial, word-processing, or typing service may find an occasional need to type a pre-printed form or application. These forms cannot be filled out using your computer. You may even carve out a niche in your market by advertising that you type forms and applications. Once the PC became commonplace in homes and offices, many companies and individuals got rid of their typewriters, certain that they would not need them again.

Postage Scale

The postage scale is a great time- and money-saver if you sometimes add extra stamps to an envelope just to be sure you have the postage covered. It also eliminates standing in line at the post office to double-check the mailing rate of a letter or package. A postage scale can mean great savings when you add up the time spent driving to the post office and standing in line. Once again, these come in various types and models, from very inexpensive to expensive. Determine how much mailing your business will be doing and let that be the guide to determining which model is best for you.

When moving to a new home, order extra address labels and send one of your personalized labels along with each change of address card to notify friends and clients of your move. They can stick the labels right in their address books.

Office Supplies

When you first start your business, you'll need to determine what office supplies are needed in order for you to work efficiently. If you previously worked at an office outside your home, make a list of the items you used regularly. If office supplies are new territory, make a list of items you know you will need to keep on hand.

Our following list will help you think of items needed for your type of business. Use our list as a starting point, then make your own personalized list. Buy in bulk whenever possible, but remember to buy in bulk only those items you need that can be used in a reasonable amount of time. For example, don't buy a case of correction fluid if you only use it one time per week. Do buy in bulk items that have a long shelf life (e.g., pencils). Here are our suggestions for basic office supplies:

- Calendar
- Computer diskettes
- Envelopes, plain
- File folders
- File labels
- Glue or rubber cement
- Index cards
- Mailing envelopes
- Mailing labels
- Paper for computer printer or copier
- Paper clips
- Pens, pencils, erasers, markers
- Binders
- Rubber bands
- Rubber stamps
- Stapler and staples
- Tape dispenser and tape (a great item to buy in bulk)
- Plastic organizer trays
- Letter opener
- Mousepad
- Paper cutter
- Pencil holder
- Postage scale
- Printer toner or ink cartridges

- Ruler(s)
- Scissors
- Staple remover

With the incredible recent growth of the home office market in this country, you now have choices and selections like never before for buying your office supplies, equipment, and furniture. Shop wisely and watch for sales and specials. Remember to buy only what you need, but make sure your office is stocked adequately so you don't waste time running out at the last minute to purchase supplies.

HOMEwork

Evaluate your office supplies, equipment, and furniture. Make a list of things you need and a list of things you want, and set goals to obtain the needed items first. For example: Buy new fax machine by December 1. Set aside twenty dollars a month for fax machine.

Chapter
Sixteen

Finding Your Customers

ach time I (Sheri) consult with a client about working at home, one of the first questions the client asks is, "How do I find my customers?" It's an important question. You may have the greatest product or service in town or you can be the best at what you do, but it doesn't mean a thing without customers. If you are currently working at home, you already know that unless you bring in customers and business you won't be working at home for long. Without work, you'll soon be out looking for a job! A nationwide survey revealed that finding the customer was one of the top 10 concerns of home-based business owners.

Try to think of time as money. You either save it or waste it, but time does cost you money.

Have you ever noticed the marketing gimmicks that retailers use at Christmas to lure customers into their stores? The day after Thanksgiving, which is famous as the biggest shopping day of the year, has become a gold mine for retailers. Storekeepers are well aware that they must do whatever it takes to get shoppers to their stores. So many offer great deals to the first 100, 500, or 1,000 shoppers in their doors. Some offer free gifts, others great discounts for a limited amount of time. Shoppers get up at 2:00 A.M. and stand in line for four hours for a chance to enter a drawing for a gift certificate or a new car. Retailers have discovered what works, and they spend a lot of money accomplishing their goal—getting the customer into the store. They have spent literally millions of research dollars finding out what customers want, and then they give it to them. You can do the same thing in your business on a much smaller scale.

You will likely be competing with others who have similar businesses. However, even if your competition is minimal, you still need to get the word out about what you have to offer, whether it is handcrafted water fountains, custom-designed T-shirts, or typing services. You must work to get your name associated with the type of business or field you've chosen. Your goal should be to ensure that everyone who needs your product or service knows about it. But that's not all. You also need to accomplish this in a way that convinces customers that they need to have your product or service.

When I (Sheri) started my typing business 20 years ago, I didn't have a great deal of competition. I was an accomplished secretary and offered the highest quality of work, but I still needed a way to reach my potential customers. And I needed to convince them that hiring an outside secretarial service would save them time and money. And just who were my customers? Here are some guidelines for you to determine who your customers are and how you can find them:

↪ Sit down and brainstorm who would benefit most from your product and/or service. Then go directly to people who would need what you have to offer. Visit potential customers who may already be using a service or product like the one you offer.

↪ Don't be afraid to get feedback about the product or service you have in mind. If you have a product available, show it to people and get their reactions. Their responses will provide you with a wealth of information at a minimal cost. If you have a service-type business, offer people a sample of it such as an article, a seminar, or a free demonstration.

↪ Will you offer a product or service that is beneficial to organizations like schools, hospitals, or large corporations? Don't be afraid to contact the organization's public relations director to schedule a meeting. Discuss the ways in which you can benefit their organization or company. Be prepared and confident.

✦ Contact other businesses that also offer your type of product or service. In other words, talk to your competition. Ask for some effective advertising methods that bring in customers. Contact companies or businesses that are located in an area which will not be in direct competition with your business. They will be much more willing to give advice and information.

✦ If you offer products, participate in trade shows, fairs, or expos and take orders. Stock up on samples of your products and literature to give to potential customers.

✦ Take the time to get feedback in the form of surveys or questionnaires. This works well for both products and services. Encourage potential customers to fill out the form in person.

General Marketing/Advertising Ideas

✦ Offer a "free" product or service for a drawing at a local function where you can meet and greet potential clients.

✦ Discover "power partners" that naturally complement your business. You can *share advertising costs* for mailers and coupons. For example, a carpet cleaning franchise and a window cleaning service or a decorating service and wallpaper-hanging service make natural pairs. You will spend half the amount on advertising and reach more potential customers because of the other company's contacts.

✦ Offer to donate samples of your product to a business for display in return for their displaying your business cards or flyers.

- Don't be shy. Talk about your business whenever you have an opening.

- Wear a professionally-designed T-shirt advertising your business with a logo and telephone number.

- Have magnetic placards made for your car that advertise your business. Their easy-on, easy-off application makes them ideal advertising pieces. Remember to always have flyers or business cards on hand in case someone asks you for information.

- Send letters and flyers to people on your block and on the neighboring blocks telling them who you are, what you do, and that you are not very far away.

- Prepare bookmarks that promote your business and ask librarians and bookshop owners to insert them with books that are checked out or purchased.

- Contact your local Chamber of Commerce to obtain a list of members. Send each member a letter about your services.

- In addition, become a member of the Chamber and attend its functions. This will help your business to become known throughout the community.

- See if you can leave several of your business cards at the Chamber of Commerce office for anyone requesting your type of service.

- Tell everyone you know and meet about your business. Word-of-mouth is the best advertiser around!

Business Cards

Business cards are one of the most effective and inexpensive methods of promoting your business. Be sure to keep in mind several guidelines when having business cards made:

- ↬ *K.I.S.S.* Keep it short and simple. Many times people fill up their business card with information that is unnecessary. A potential customer will look at your business card for three seconds—yes three seconds! Make sure that your business card reflects only the necessary information:

    —Business name.

    —Your name and business address. Use caution when listing your home address on the card. You might have customers who show up without an appointment! Have half of the cards printed with the address and half without.

    —Telephone number (large enough to read).

    —Other pertinent numbers such as fax, pager, etc.

    —A simple one-line sentence or phrase giving a brief description of what services or products you provide (if it isn't clear in your business name).

- ↬ Use top-quality paper and have your cards typeset and printed professionally. Sometimes a business card will make your very first impression on a potential client. Make sure it is a good one. If your telephone number changes, have new cards printed. It looks very unprofessional to cross out and handwrite a new number.

- Use a rubber stamp to list your E-mail or website address. If these addresses change (and they often do), you won't have to have new cards printed. A rubber stamp costs less than 10 dollars and is a great investment.

Using Your Business Cards for Marketing

- With the manager's permission, leave several business cards at local office supply stores.

- Give business cards to your friends and acquaintances. They can also pass them along to others who may be in need of your services.

- Mail your business card and information to every post office box in the local post office. (You might want to get a price quote first.)

- Include your business card with the bills you pay to local companies. Your unique style of advertising will be an interesting conversation opener.

- With permission, leave your business cards and information at local hotels, motels, inns, and bed-and-breakfasts. Out-of-town guests may need your service or product and will be grateful to find you.

- Attach your business cards to community bulletin boards in your area.

- See if you can place your business cards in local restaurants.

- Visit local laundromats, car washes, and other establishments where customers often stand around for long periods of time. Display your business cards on any available bulletin boards.

Keep a pad of paper and pen next to your bed and in your bathroom. Jot down ideas, things to do, supplies to get, new marketing or advertising ideas to try, etc.

↜ Add your business cards to bulletin boards on college campuses.

↜ Distribute your business card and information to area beauty salons and barbershops. Many times the owners are willing to help promote local businesses.

And always remember to carry a large supply of business cards with you every time you leave your house. Keep a supply in your car. You never know when someone will request information on your business. By being prepared and organized, you will give the impression of success.

Another way to use business cards effectively is to collect cards from other businesses and individuals to use as a client/customer mailing list. As soon as you have entered the information on the business card into the computer, throw it away. It's amazing how fast business cards can pile up into additional paper clutter. There are some incredibly simple computer programs on the market that allow you to make database files for your customers and potential customers. Check with your favorite computer store to find which would work best for your business.

Other Methods for Marketing and Advertising

There are many avenues in which you can market your business, and our list is certainly far from complete. However, you will find some practical ideas here to get your creative juices flowing. Take an idea that suits your personality, then try it!

Networking

One of the most popular ways to market and advertise your business is by networking. This can be done both formally and informally. Networking is the same thing as "word-of-mouth" advertising. Some formal networking can be found through your local Chamber of Commerce or individual business networking groups. I (Sheri) belong to a great local networking group, Let's Network, which meets one morning a week for breakfast. Fees are very reasonable and, because memberships are exclusive (only one from each type of business), I have the opportunity to share about my business with 40–50 other local business owners each week. I keep my business in front of the members and let them know how they can refer clients to me. I also reward members of my networking group with special discounts on my services for referrals. Let's Network has a website that gives information regarding rules and guidelines as well as a member list (www.letsnetwork.com). The purpose of the network is to generate referrals or "leads" for other members in the group.

Families and friends are probably the oldest networks of all. A word-of-mouth referral by someone who knows you and your business is the best kind of referral. Make sure family members and friends have plenty of your business cards on hand to give to potential clients when they are talking about your business and what you do.

Volunteering

Volunteering is one of the best ways to get your name out to a large group of people with a minimal amount of expense. Volunteering your time and energy in exchange for mention of your business in a program or newsletter is an excellent way to promote your at-home business. People like working with companies that are willing to give time, money, or products to worthy causes.

Packaging Your Products

When selecting packaging for your products, remember that it can be a "business card" of sorts. If products are packaged with quality and creativity, you will at the least be guaranteed a second look. Check out your competition and see how their products are packaged, then determine how to improve your own presentation.

Referrals

Referrals are your best form of advertising. When clients or customers who have used your service or purchased your product refer you to

Use a pencil to write phone numbers and addresses in your address book. If someone moves, you can easily make the necessary changes without messing up your book.

friends, coworkers, or family members, they are saying that you have a superior product or provide an excellent service. No better advertising can be found than a great referral. Don't forget to reward your referring clients with a thank-you offering of a great discount on a product or service.

Donating to Charities

By donating products and/or services to charities, you once again allow yourself to get your name out to the public. Name recognition is essential to becoming successful. You may not receive a referral that materializes into a client or customer for several months. Don't wait for them to contact you. Call and offer your service or product and give them a number to contact you when they are ready to do business with you.

Quality Letterhead and Business Cards

Don't pinch pennies in the area of your letterhead and business cards. Spend the necessary money to have your letterhead professionally typeset and printed. The quality of your letterhead and business cards speaks volumes about the quality of work your business provides. Remember, you rarely get a second chance to make a good first impression.

Publicity in Newspapers, Magazines, Radio and Television, and Trade Publications

Carefully research which avenues of publicity will work best for you. Check with businesses that do the same kind of work you do. Ask what works, and then use it. Keep in mind that this type of advertising is expensive and needs to be carefully researched and well-thought out before you invest your resources.

Product Samples

What better way to get your product in front of the customer than to offer free samples? Use them as giveaways whenever possible. Of course, larger and more expensive items should be used sparingly, perhaps as drawing prizes for community gatherings and special events.

Newsletters

If you offer consulting services, a newsletter is a great way to offer advice and keep clients up-to-date with what is going on in your business. This way, you also keep your name in front of them. For example, a bookkeeping/tax service could send quarterly newsletters updating clients on new tax law changes and a checklist for year-end tax preparations.

Flyers

Flyers are an excellent way to advertise your business specials and let your customers know of any changes or additions to your services or products. Offer discounts (seasonal?) to attract new customers.

Brochures

A professional brochure can save you time by explaining exactly what services and/or products you have to offer. Once again, quality is the key. Time- and money-saving tip: Don't list prices on the brochure, especially if you are spending the money to print four-color brochures. Prices change often, so design a separate price list to be inserted with the brochure when sending it out. Print the price list with black ink on white paper.

Trade Shows and Exhibits for Product Demonstrations

If your business offers products, promote it by purchasing "space" at trade shows and exhibits that will allow you to demonstrate what products you offer. Efficient demonstration of your product and how to use it will only enhance its sales appeal. Have on hand order forms and plenty of flyers and business cards.

Direct Mail

Direct mail can either be a winner or a loser. Direct mail is anything that is mailed through the U.S. Postal Service and includes "coupon" envelopes, letters, cards, bulk mail, etc. Because every business is different, some will see a great return with direct mail, others won't. Once again check out the market for your product and/or service to see if direct mail will work for you. Make sure your mailing list is current and up-to-date. Double-check to see that names are spelled correctly when entering them into your database. The extra time spent on this will reap benefits down the road. Most people surveyed said that if junk mail was addressed incorrectly, had a name spelled wrong, or was addressed to "occupant," it was thrown out without even being opened.

Classified Ads in Newspapers and Magazines

Some businesses do well with classified advertising, but keep in mind that this is generally quite expensive. You might share this advertising vehicle with a business that complements your business. You divide the cost in half and still reach the same number of potential customers. Ads need to be well written, short, and to-the-point. We advise you to get professional help in writing your ad.

Yellow Page Advertising

Yellow page advertising is a great way to advertise both product and service businesses. Once again, some businesses have great success with yellow page advertising and others find it doesn't give enough return for their monthly investment. I (Sheri) find that 90% of my cold-calling customers come from my yellow page advertising. It is my most successful means of reaching new customers. Even if you don't receive a high percentage of customers from your yellow page ad, remember that it does signify a successful and professional business.

Fax and E-Mail

One of the newest forms of mass advertising is via the fax machine and electronic mail (E-mail). Once thought of as a tool to move important documents very quickly, the fax machine has become extremely successful in advertising tool. However, keep in mind that many consumers find fax advertising annoying and a waste of paper. Be sure to offer a way for customers to be eliminated from the mass number mailing if they so desire.

Web Pages

Another growing medium for marketing and advertising is utilizing the Internet to create an advertising page known as a "web page." Use a reputable company and ask for references. Be careful of offers that are inexpensive or "free." There may be hidden charges.

There are many resources available with great ideas and tips for marketing and advertising. You can find dozens of books and audiotapes to choose from that offer even more ways to market and advertise your at-home business. Audiotapes are wonderful if you spend a good deal of time in the car. For more information, visit your local bookstore or library.

HOMEwork

Head to your local bookstore or library and select at least one book on marketing. Read one chapter a day until you have completed the book. Next, choose five marketing ideas that you would like to implement and write them in the "goals" section of your planner. Give specific dates for when you will begin using each idea for your business. Record which ideas are successful and which are not.

Talent Meets Perseverance

The Sellers Family
John, Lisa, and children

When Lisa Sellers married her husband, John, she became instant "Mom" to his three beautiful children Ricky, Michael, and Jaime. She was a great stepmom, though she never considered herself to be particularly maternal. Three years after John and Lisa were married, they discovered that they were expecting a child. The moment their son Shaun was born, those deep motherly instincts created a whole new personality in Lisa. She no longer wanted to return to work as a dispatcher for the Highway Patrol after her four-month maternity leave was over. She began to realize the importance of being home with her son and the two stepchildren who had come to live full-time with the family. After reluctantly returning to work, Lisa began to look for stay-at-home alternatives, brainstorming ways to be at home with the kids and use her talents to help the family financially.

Then God blessed Lisa with an opportunity to begin a business of cleaning model homes for new housing tracts. She and her crew would clean 15 model homes twice a week. They would begin at 5:00 P.M. when the models closed, travel 108 miles round trip, and get back home around midnight. (This was in addition to her full-time job.) The money was good and helped the family to pay off quite a few bills. However, with a small baby and two preteens at home, Lisa realized that she needed to reconsider her options. John calculated some figures and estimated that Lisa could quit her full-time job as a dispatcher in approximately four months. Though the hours spent working both jobs were long, the dream of being a full-time mom kept her going. It was a complete thrill when John told her that they were ahead of schedule with their savings plan and she could quit her job in only three months. And she did! It was scary to take the leap, but they were motivated. Shortly after that, Lisa was able to discontinue her model home cleaning business.

Lisa loved being a full-time mom to her brood, but it turned out that one income was not enough to pay the bills. So Lisa and John decided to try another avenue of earning additional income. When Shaun was two years old, Lisa decided to open her own secretarial service. She had learned a great deal about computers and word processing at her previous full-time job. As well, she was a very talented typist and had good business skills. She already owned a high-quality computer and printer, so with a small investment for a phone line and answering machine, she was ready for business.

Lisa was also helped along the way by a mentor. She was able to save a lot of time by having someone to turn to when she needed information. She started her business with overflow work from a local secretarial service and in the meantime began to build up her own clientele. She now has several regular customers and has many marketing strategies to explore as the funds become available. As with any business, Lisa knows that if she perseveres and keeps her eyes on God, the blessings will continue to overflow.

Chapter
Seventeen

Money Matters: Deciding How Much to Charge

Okay, so you have a great idea for a business or a dynamite product to sell. Now how much do you charge for your product or service? This is one of the most frequently asked questions from prospective home-based business owners. And if you ask several different business "professionals" for their opinion, you'll get several different answers ranging from, "You have to be the lowest price your customers can find," to "Charge as much as you can get." But just what is "as much as you can get?" Your rates really are one of the most difficult decisions involved in starting a business. Getting people to part with their money is an art. They work hard to earn it and they want to make sure they are getting something for their dollar. But have you ever noticed that when people really want something badly, they will pay almost any amount of money to get it? The secret is to get customers to want (and value) your product or service badly enough to pay your asking price for it.

When I (Sheri) started my typing service, I was fortunate that the only other typing service in town was more than willing to give me time-tested advice on the going rate for such services. It would have been extremely difficult for me to determine prices on my own simply because I had nothing to gauge them against. When I (Emilie) started doing More Hours In My Day seminars, Bob and I took advice from others in the consulting field. We then combined that information with Bob's business knowledge and expertise to come up with a cost that was both reasonable to the attendee and allowed me to receive the money I was worth as a speaker.

One of the biggest mistakes in pricing a product or service for a home-based business is selling yourself short and charging too little. But charging too much can be just as counterproductive. So how do you find the happy medium in pricing?

The specific elements of real order include a home that is easy to move around in, with simple systems of dealing with the handling of paperwork and money management.

Do Your Homework

If you choose a business that has adequate market saturation, you will be forced to stay within certain parameters for pricing. However, by nature many home-based businesses are more personalized and customized than other businesses and therefore will have more leeway in setting prices. Ask yourself the following questions to help you determine just what your business product or service is worth:

1. *How much is your product or service worth?*

Answers will vary tremendously based on where you live, how many like businesses exist in your area, and what demand consumers have for your product or service. Will your product or service save money or produce money for your potential customer/client?

2. *What will potential clients/customers pay?*

It doesn't matter how wonderful your holiday gift baskets are; if people won't pay what you are asking or they can get them cheaper somewhere else, then you must reevaluate your asking price. Your perception of what your product or service is worth is just as important as its actual value. On the other hand, charging too little for your product or service can also hurt business. If clients perceive your product or service as too cheap, they may not do business with you. They might assume you haven't been in business long enough or can't compete in quality or customer service. I (Sheri) often have potential customers call and ask for my résumé prices. I quote my rates and if they say the price is too high, I suggest they contact other resume services in the area for a comparison. I then advise them to make sure a cheaper resume service has the proper background and experience for writing and designing resumes. I encourage them to shop around, knowing I am well within the going rate for my services. Nine out of 10 times, the client calls me back and I get the job.

Ask friends and family members what they would pay for your product or service. Get honest feedback. Talk to as many people as you can to realistically determine your rates.

3. Are you charging enough to make money?

Remember that you are in business to make money! Will you have more money coming in than going out? If not, you may need to reevaluate what you are charging or find ways to cut some of your costs and overhead expenses. Remember that your direct costs (time, materials, etc.) plus your overhead (advertising, utilities, administrative costs, etc.) plus your profit equal the price you need to charge for your product or service. Listed below are some examples of direct costs and overhead expenses.

Direct Costs for the Project	Overhead Expenses
Telephone calls for the task	Advertising/Marketing
Copies made for the task	Office equipment
Outside typing service	Business telephone service/fax
Postage	Health insurance
Special materials or supplies needed	Utilities
Your salary	Employee benefits
Travel and lodging	Office supplies

Simple Guidelines to Product or Service Pricing

Many pricing principles are the same for either a product or service; however, some elements in pricing a product differ from those involved in setting up pricing for a service-based business. One of the biggest differences is that most service businesses have very few direct costs of doing business. However, when you sell a product, you must pay for your product or the supplies to make it up front and keep an inventory on hand for orders.

When pricing a product you'll need to consider manufacturing costs, determine and set wholesale prices compared to retail prices, and figure in provision for markups and discounts. According to authors and home business experts Paul and Sarah Edwards, many home-based business owners use the following formula to determine an initial price for their products:

total material costs + overhead + minimum profit + retail margin = retail price[9]

Service businesses can be priced several different ways—hourly, by the day, by the project or task, or by the piece. Check with others in your particular type of business. They can be

Beware of the "tail wagging the dog" syndrome. Avoid situations in which the appointment book, the budget and expenditure records, the filing system, and the master list take more time to maintain than working out the problems they're supposed to solve.

the best source of information. Many types of businesses have national organizations that publish a guideline for determining pricing. For example, the National Association of Secretarial Services (NASS) publishes an annual booklet to help its members determine pricing for their businesses. You must be a member to receive this information.

Publisher Hal Schuster (of Simon & Schuster) had this to say about pricing: Your fair price is the price point at which you can maintain sufficient business. Raise your prices slowly at intervals until you find a manageable point in your workload. Then stop raising them. Then if you are consistently attracting more business than you can handle, you can raise them again.[10]

A Simple Step-by-Step Pricing Guide

Although no one pricing formula will work for everyone, Paul and Sarah Edwards offer the following process for determining what approach might work best for you at a given time:

1. Work out several possible pricing strategies.

2. Test each alternative with several prospective clients.

3. Select the alternative that gets the best response.

4. Remember, pricing is an experimental process, so continue fine-tuning until you're satisfied with the results.

5. Keep track of your income and expenses and evaluate your pricing every quarter. Make changes when the numbers or any of the following indicate the need to adjust:

   ↬ Many complaints about your price.

↪ Many other complaints that may be dissatisfaction with your price in disguise.

↪ A downturn in sales or the fact that people lost interest after hearing the price.

↪ People saying, "Boy, that's a bargain."

↪ Your prices have been the same for a long period of time.

↪ You're turning away business because you don't have time to do it.

↪ Sales are fine but profits are low.

↪ You feel resentful about working so hard for so little return.

Pricing is like the pulse of your business. When it's working, you're working. And that means that life's working.[11]

HOMEwork

Evaluate your pricing structure. See if any changes need to be made in order for you to work more efficiently in less time and make more money. Set a timetable to reevaluate your pricing structure in three months. Make any necessary changes.

Chapter
Eighteen

Bookkeeping, Taxes, and Insurance

One of the areas that you need to think about when making the decision to work at home is the effect it will have on your family's income and your taxes. You also need to consider how you will handle the bookkeeping end of your business. There is no steadfast rule here. Our best advice is to decide in your planning stage what system works best for your type of business and your lifestyle.

I (Sheri) interviewed my tax accountant/bookkeeper, Shirley Taylor of Taylor Business Group, while researching material for this book. Shirley gives the following guidelines for determining if you need a bookkeeping service and/or a professional tax preparer for your year-end business tax returns.

⁓ It is advisable to at least consider hiring a tax preparer and bookkeeper when starting your business. At the very minimum, set up a one-time consultation with a reputable firm to discuss what documents are important and necessary for your type of business along with what must be saved and what can be thrown out. A professional can also give you educated advice on how long to save business documents in your office or storage area. Most reputable firms generally offer this free consultation. Check with other businesses in your area, your local Chamber of Commerce, and friends to find the firms in your area that have the best reputation. Business and personal referrals generally work best to help you choose an accounting/tax service.

⁓ To determine what business documents, records, and receipts you need to keep, contact a professional for advice about what you need to save and store. Keep all business receipts and documents in one place, completely separate from your household documents, preferably in a vinyl or plastic bag with a snap or zipper so you avoid losing any important paperwork. Keep bank statements and canceled checks together along with check stubs and register receipts. Organize invoices, receipts for purchases, and cash receipts in a manner that suits your personality type. Once a month you need to deliver your paperwork to your bookkeeper if you choose to use this service.

⁓ When considering the cost of a bookkeeper, determine whether the time you spend organizing your books and records would be better spent marketing your business. In the beginning your business will be smaller and therefore the bookkeeping will be simpler. Every three months sit down and determine if it is time to let a bookkeeping firm handle your paperwork. If paperwork is taking more than an average of one-to-two hours per week, you may want to consider using a bookkeeping service.

↬ There are some incredible tax advantages to working at home. But beware! This is an area where you will spend your money wisely if you let a reputable tax preparer handle your year-end taxes. They always keep current on new legislation, and in the area of home-based businesses, those laws are changing every day. Each business is different and requires a knowledgeable professional to make sure you are getting the best tax advice possible. If your home office or designated area is used solely for your business, you are allowed a deduction based on square footage whether you are renting or buying your home or apartment. You need to discuss this write-off with someone who is well-versed in the law. As well, you are allowed deductions in the following areas:

—telephone expenses (business line only and only for business transactions)

—a portion of your utilities

—repairs and maintenance to your home

—car expenses and mileage

The point we're making here is that you really cannot begin to know all the possible deductions and tax breaks that are available to you. It is important to start your business on solid ground. Because every business is different,

Why does a half-hour job often take twice as long as you thought it would? Probably because you estimated only the actual working time and didn't take into account the preparation— getting out and putting away tools, for instance.

you may have expenses and write-offs that are unique to your type of business. What can be deducted from one business may not be deductible for another. A home-based business that starts off with a reputation for fairness, honesty, and integrity will go far. Be careful of costly mistakes and bad advice. If something sounds too good to be true, it probably is.[12]

Business Insurance

Did you know that just as car insurance is required in order to register and drive a vehicle, business insurance is also required for home-based businesses? The laws and requirements vary from county to county and state to state. Keep in mind that the insurance you purchase will benefit both you and your business. It will protect you in case of fire, theft, natural disaster, liability, disability, or health problems. Every state is different, so we recommend contacting an agent or carrier to discuss your insurance needs and costs. As we stated earlier, laws in favor of home-based businesses are changing almost daily. By spending time researching information, you will be able to find a policy that fits your needs and those of your business.

If you can answer yes to any of the following questions, you need to consider obtaining special insurance for your home-based business:

1. Will you *ever* receive customers/clients at your home office?

2. Will you ever be carrying business equipment or products in your car while traveling for business?

3. Does your existing policy cover office equipment at home that is used exclusively for the business? If so, how much coverage is allowed? You will need to make sure that insurance for computer equipment covers replacement costs and not just the cost of what you paid for your equipment. A good rule of thumb is to take several pictures and/or video of your office and any special equipment you have, particularly if your business has equipment that is unique or unusual, such as scientific or specialized camera equipment. It is a good idea to take pictures of your home and belongings as well in case of a fire or other natural disaster. It makes the replacement process much quicker and a whole lot easier for both you and your agent.

4. Does your policy cover data losses for your business if lost to a fire or flood?

One of the wisest investments you can make working at home is a fireproof safe. The old saying "An ounce of prevention is worth a pound of cure" is accurate. My (Sheri's) husband, Tim, is a firefighter who sees firsthand the total devastation fire causes. He has watched as irreplaceable items literally went up in smoke, and he often spends time consoling families as they face the long and arduous ordeal

To protect valuable mementos and records from fire or flood—and to keep them all in one place as well— store them in a metal strongbox or a small footlocker.

of trying to replace lost items. By spending money now on the purchase of a good fireproof safe, you may be saving literally thousands of dollars at the very least, as well as many valuable hours of time.

Paul and Sarah Edwards, authors of several excellent home-based business books, have listed some insurance rules to consider:

Insurance Rule of Thumb #1:

Only risk what you can afford to lose.

Insurance Rule of Thumb #2:

Assume you need it unless you can find proof you actually don't.

Insurance Rule of Thumb #3:

Never assume you're covered for business purposes on any personal policy. If you are doing any business in your home, have your existing insurance reviewed by a knowledgeable insurance professional to see what risks involved in your business activities are not covered.

Insurance Rule of Thumb #4:

Phase in your insurance as you grow, adding additional coverage as your profits increase.

Insurance Rule of Thumb #5:

The right agent can probably find what you need. Expect results or change agents until you get them.[13]

Health Insurance

Health insurance is a relatively new concept in the United States, as it did not begin until the 1920s. Up to that time, most people worked at home and the need for health insurance was unheard of. If they got sick or injured they went to the doctor and paid for his services. Today, however, health care is a hot topic with changes occurring daily.

What does this mean for the home-based business owner? Many of you haven't considered health insurance for your business either because you are currently covered by a spouse's insurance and/or you have no employees who make health coverage a necessary consideration. However, we have discovered that many home-based businesses are now made up of husband/wife teams who have no health insurance for themselves or their children.

Health insurance for the self-employed is now big business. Insurance companies are watching the trends and are beginning to offer packages that are reasonably priced and include great coverage.

In the early 1990s, Congress passed a law which stated that small businesses (including home-based businesses) must have the same opportunities as large companies and corporations. It is now possible for "group" insurance to be offered to a small business, which is classified as two people operating the business. This can be a husband/wife, father/son, father/daughter, mother/son, or mother/daughter team. Every major insurance company in the United States now offers a group plan for small business. They have seen the opportunity to make money and are now offering several plans to make it possible to obtain health insurance. What are the requirements for "small business" status for your home-based business?

- ↬ You must have a valid business license.

- ↬ You must be a full-time business. (You must work a minimum of 20 hours in the business to be considered full-time.)

What are the benefits of small group insurance versus individual coverage?

- ↬ No medical underwriting required.

- ↬ Simple form.

- ↬ Low-cost coverage (cost is dependent on your age and geographical location—every state is different).

Every state has a Department of Insurance. This is a great place to start if you have questions. This is also the place to contact if you need to file a complaint.

Every major insurance company also has a toll-free number and should be more than willing to give you information over the telephone. The company can arrange for an agent in your area to give you information and answer any questions.

Nancy Dunham, an independent insurance agent with Affordable Health Care, suggests considering the following questions when searching for health insurance:

1. What are your health care needs? Do you visit the doctor only one time a year for checkups? If so, why pay for doctor visits in your policy? Skip the doctor benefit and take only lab and in-hospital coverage.

2. Do you use a lot of prescriptions? Evaluate the prescription section of the policy. Some pay 80%, some

offer a $10 co-payment, some offer no prescription benefits at all. Determine which is best for you and your family.

3. Will an indemnity plan or an HMO work best for you? You will have greater choices with respect to doctors and medical facilities with an indemnity plan; however, your expense will be greater. With an HMO, there are fewer choices but the packages are much more reasonable costwise.

4. Research brokers or agents who offer multiple choices in plans, then interview them to make them aware of your preferences and needs, and let them do the work for you. This is what they are paid to do. If they don't want to do the research, find another agent or broker who will.

5. You can go directly to the insurance company in which you are interested for information. They will gladly send you packets with information about what their particular company offers. Blue Shield and Blue Cross are national companies. Kaiser Permanente and PacifiCare are basically West Coast companies.

6. If you or a member of your family has a serious disabling disorder such as diabetes or multiple sclerosis, check with the Department of Insurance in your state for information on state high-risk plans.

Remember to do your homework and gather as much information as possible. You can't ask too many questions. Get information from at least three different companies so that you will have plenty of material to compare. Ask your friends, coworkers, neighbors, and family members about their health care coverage. They will generally tell you immediately whether or not they are happy with it.

There are other types of insurance you might be interested in such as property insurance, disability insurance, and life insurance. Discuss these first with your spouse and then with a professional to determine what is best for you and your family.

HOMEwork

Any system of organization must be right for you. There is no best way to be organized. Whatever methods you select, make sure they fit your lifestyle and business needs.

Chapter
Nineteen

Dressing
for Success

The cliché "You never get a second chance to make a good first impression" especially holds true when you are working at a home business. Simply because you are working at home, you must give the impression that you are a professional. When a client comes to a home business, he or she has already determined that the business must be small and modestly successful. How you dress is vitally important to delivering a great impression of success, quality, and professionalism. Most people assume that if you work at home, your dress will be more casual and informal. For this reason it is imperative that what you wear

It's important to look professional and not weighted down when making customer calls. Invest in one leather briefcase that holds your wallet, makeup, calendar, and other business-related files. If you go to lunch and you don't want to take your briefcase, simply take your wallet and go. No more fumbling with briefcase, purse, keys, etc.

speaks volumes about the quality of goods or services you provide.

In my (Sheri's) typing business, dressing professionally directly correlates to the quality of the typing I provide. If my office is messy or cluttered or if I greet customers at the door wearing my old sweats and a baggy shirt, prospective clients may decide that the quality of my work reflects my messy presentation. However, in the very early morning hours I am able to complete a great deal of typing while dressed in sweats and slippers. My office hours are well-defined and I am not worried about clients showing up at 5:00 A.M.

Think for a minute about a place of business that you deal with on a regular basis. Does it make a difference to you what the workers are wearing? Of course it does. If the woman behind the makeup counter at Nordstrom were wearing jeans and an old rock star T-shirt, wouldn't you think twice about allowing her to wait on you? If you go into a corporate office setting, you don't expect to find employees dressed in jeans and sweatshirts. In the same way you want your dress to reflect the professional image you are trying to present. The more professional your style, the more professional your business. Jo, a Mary Kay consultant who works from home, is always dressed attractively with her makeup impeccable. She is a walking business card. She would never think of leaving her home in old clothes and no makeup. As well, her hairstyle is modern and stylish. She never knows when she will meet a prospective client so she takes every opportunity to put her best foot forward.

When I (Sheri) started my typing service, working at home was still a novelty. Very few home businesses existed and those that did were met with suspicion. On several occasions once a customer discovered the business was home-based, he or she canceled the appointment. They assumed that something had to be wrong if I was working at home instead of in an office setting.

It is very easy to fall into the trap of reasoning, "I'm just at home—my customer or client won't mind what I'm wearing." To a small degree, this is true. However, keep in mind that you may also be sending a negative message to a customer or client.

Obviously, some home business occupations require very casual dress. It would be ridiculous for a woodcrafter to greet customers wearing a suit. On the other hand, a medical transcriptionist who sees doctors needs to project an extremely professional image to her clients. Our friend Debbie and her husband own a home-based computer business. He builds and repairs computers, and she is in charge of marketing and sales. They do not see customers at their home, but when she makes prospective client calls Debbie dresses accordingly.

Another determining factor for your dress is whether or not you have children. Lisa, who owns a word-processing business, has an active two-year-old. When customers come for appointments at her home office, she changes into a casual dress to greet them. Once they leave, she changes back into more comfortable clothes. Lisa works more effectively in casual clothes but also wants to present a professional image to her clients. She is careful to schedule appointments together in the same block of time to minimize clothing changes.

As you figure out what type of dress is best for your business, ask yourself some questions to help determine what is best for both comfort and image:

1. Will you receive customers at your home?

2. Will you deliver products to or provide services for clients in their homes or places of business?

There are several excellent reasons for dressing in a professional manner if you'll be working at home.

1. Your professional dress conveys a positive message to your customers. As well, you are starting your day in a positive frame of mind.

2. By showering and dressing early in the morning you start your day ready to take on any challenges that come your way. You will save time by not having to stop mid-morning and change clothes.

3. You won't need to rush and change if an unexpected client calls and needs to stop by. You will eliminate the stress of frantic showering and/or changing at the last minute.

HOMEwork

Take a critical look at your wardrobe this week. Decide which outfits are appropriate for your professional look and what you may need to purchase to complete an outfit or pull together an existing few pieces of clothing.

Growing with the Baby

The Acevedo Family
Roland, Trina, and Baby Kyle

Shortly after Thanksgiving in 1997, Roland and Trina Acevedo found out they were going to be parents. Roland, a deputy sheriff for almost 10 years, and Trina, a full-time merchandise assistant and part-time student, knew there was no conceivable way to keep up their busy lifestyle. Trina wanted to continue with school, but she also wanted to be able to stay home with the baby. And she still had a desire to contribute to the family income.

Trina eagerly started researching how to begin a home business, particularly a typing business. She was very interested in typing based on her extensive background and education in computers. Her mother gave her a book on how to start a home business, and the book provided Trina with excellent information about what she needed to know. The process of searching for information and finding it was extremely encouraging to her. She knew her idea would work if she put in the required effort. Her confidence level increased as she continued her research. Her motivation was the thought of being able to be home to see all of their baby's "firsts."

After gathering information and advice, Trina began to purchase equipment and supplies, using money she had saved from her job before she went on maternity leave. She knew that when she no longer had a regular paycheck, her essential equipment would already be purchased. The Acevedos worked hard to set up a functional office area in their home. They converted a formal dining room to Trina's office, and she was ready to begin. She was excited because she knew this would be a change for the better and a chance to really see what she could accomplish on her own.

The moment Kyle was born, Trina knew she didn't want to work outside the home. She wanted to be the person who cared for their baby, and being able to stay at home was a dream come true.

Trina and Roland discovered that money wasn't as important to them as Trina's being "mommy" to Kyle. But being able to supplement the family income is great for her. Because she was able to start her business while she was pregnant, she will be able to watch her son grow up and know that her business will grow each year as he grows.

Chapter
Twenty

Working in the Neighborhood

O ne of your greatest sources of support can be your neighbors. If you have relied on a neighbor for an extra cup of sugar or a ride to the market, consider yourself fortunate to live next to such helpful people. So how do you work with these neighbors in relation to a home-based business? It is important to find out how the people around you feel about your working at home. If you know your neighbors well, follow these simple guidelines and you'll continue your good relationships with them:

1. **Communication:** Inform neighbors immediately once you make the decision to work at home.

2. **Reassurance:** Assure them that noise and traffic will be kept to a minimum.

3. **Maintenance:** Keep your lawn well-maintained, your house in good repair and freshly painted, your trees and shrubs trimmed, etc. Nothing will eliminate neighbor support for your business quicker than a home and yard that are not well-maintained.

4. **Reminder:** Remind them that you will be happy to keep an eye on the neighborhood while they are away at work.

5. **Sensitivity:** Be sensitive to the environmental concerns that impact the neighborhood. Will your business generate increased noise levels or produce unhealthy air from machinery usage? Will traffic increase? Will you be able to limit the number of vehicles at your house at one time? Will you be operating loud machinery late in the evening?

6. **Freebies:** Offer your products and/or services free or at a greatly reduced price. I (Sheri) offer free typing to any neighbors (within reason) needing that service. I have also prepared resumes for several neighbors and enjoy being able to provide them with this service.

In the event that your business may require a variance or special zoning permits, it will be much easier to acquire needed signatures from your neighbors if you have worked at developing a relationship with them over time.

If for some reason you have neighbors who are opposed to your home-based business, take their concerns very seriously. Respond to them from a positive point of view and do not get defensive. Be prepared to offer your personal guarantee that the areas of concern will be addressed and fixed.

The key here is sharing information. If you don't let your neighbors know what you are doing, you risk raising concern and speculation about what is going on in your home. When my (Sheri's) family moved to our current home, Tim took off several weeks from work to get the house in order. My typing service was busier than ever and I was seeing a number of clients each day. Several weeks after we moved in, one of the neighbors came to our house and introduced himself. After chatting for awhile, Tim mentioned that I had a home-based word-processing service and would be seeing clients at home. He assured the neighbor that the traffic would be minimal and that no more than one client would come at a time. The neighbor began laughing. After seeing the puzzled look on Tim's face, he said he was glad to know a legitimate business was generating all that traffic. Since he had not seen Tim leaving for work and noticed that he'd been staying at home all day, the neighbor was sure that we must have been operating a drug business out of our house. Everyone had a good laugh, but the story serves as a good reminder of the importance of informing neighbors about what you are doing. It can alleviate possible unfounded fears and keep misunderstandings to a minimum.

Home Security

Many husbands who have wives wanting to start at-home businesses ask us lots of questions about home security— Will my wife be safe if she has clients coming to the home? What precautions can I take to minimize risks? We have come up with some precautions you can take to be as safe as possible. This list is certainly not all-inclusive, but it gives you some ideas.

- ✦ Don't take a client to an upstairs office. Place a small desk near your entryway to greet customers and take orders or receive work.

- ✦ Keep a small canister of pepper spray at your desk for precaution. Keep it completely up and away if your children are younger than 12.

- ✦ Use your natural intuition. If someone on the telephone doesn't sound right or makes you feel uneasy, make sure you have someone with you when that customer arrives. Or schedule appointments when your husband, a friend, or a neighbor can be in your office at home with you.

- ✦ Keep your doors locked while working at home. Make sure to lock your doors when leaving, even if only for just a few minutes.

- ✦ Purchase a home security system. Many companies offer free or greatly reduced installation and equipment costs when you sign a monitoring contract. The monthly fee is less expensive than cable television.

- ✦ Get a large dog that barks at strangers. Our local police department assures us that barking dogs are the best deterrent against burglars.

- ✦ Light up your outside premises well. You can't have too many lights around your home. Make sure your motion-activated sensor lighting has a detector that projects straight down in case of someone edging along the outside wall.

- Hire a housesitter when you will be gone. College students, grandparents, or aunts and uncles are good choices.

- Have someone pick up newspapers and mail while you are gone.

- When you are gone, give the appearance that someone is home. Continue with your regular lawn service, and keep your lawn sprinklers on automatic. You can purchase timers for your interior lights so that they will turn on and off. Use timers in several rooms of the house.

- Do not change your answering machine message to let customers know you will be gone. Inform your regular customers personally of the days your office will be closed. Turn your phone down to low or completely off until you return.

- Consider instigating a neighborhood watch program. Contact your local police department for the proper way to begin a patrol watch for your area.

- Make sure that all smoke detectors are working and have fresh batteries. Pick a date such as January 1 to change the batteries whether they need it or not. You will be assured they will always be in working order.

- Remember, you probably were at a much greater risk walking from your office to the car when you worked outside your home. By utilizing common sense and a few precautions, you will be safe while working at home.

HOMEwork

When you are away on vacation or are away from your home for a period of time:

1. Instruct the post office to hold your mail until you return.

2. Stop deliveries of paper, milk, and so forth.

3. Buy a timer and hook it up so that a light goes on at dusk and off at midnight.

4. Inform a trusted neighbor that you will be away and have him or her look after your home.

5. Invite a friend or college student to stay at your house while you are away.

Ideas for Working at Home

Here we've included over 100 easy business ideas for women that can be started with little training and investment. All of these ideas are capable of producing additional income.

Most of these businesses can be conducted in the privacy and comfort of your home, in between household chores, during weekends, or at your leisure. All of these ideas do not require extra help and, best of all, some are extensions of hobbies or skills you have been developing or acquiring since childhood.

For best results, browse through the business ideas and write down those that sound interesting. List the opportunities you would like to try out. Then narrow the list down to one, two, or more related businesses. For instance, if you collect dolls as a hobby, you can start you own doll making business or start designing and sewing doll clothes (perhaps specializing in party clothes) for Barbies or Cabbage Patch Kids.

These ideas are intended to stimulate your imagination. Only you can make the decision based on your own experiences, qualifications, interests, and the current market in your community. As you compile your list of possibilities, take a critical look around your area and note what is and isn't available, the quality of products or services, and the going rates for these businesses, and do some research. When you find just the right combination, start preparing to have a successful at-home business!

Adult Day Care Center. Operate a center to look after elderly and/or handicapped people. Offer refreshments, games, activities, and assistance, but not health care.

Advertising Specialties. With distributor-provided catalogs and samples, call on regular customers and supply them with custom imprinted pens, calendars, matches, etc.

It all comes down to a place for everything and everything in its place—just as soon as it comes into the house! Otherwise, you'll put it somewhere "for now," but it will really be forever.

Advertising Service. Arrange for the design, printing, and distribution of advertising announcement flyers, mailouts, and ad campaigns for clients. Charge a fee plus commission.

African Violets. Specialize in the propagation and care of this popular indoor plant. Hybridize and sell when in full bloom, and also sell accessories and supplies.

Alterations. Replace buttons, let out cuffs, shorten sleeves, turn collars, and repair tears for clothing stores, laundromats, and cleaners who don't already offer this service.

Aquarium Snails. Raise red ramshorn snails for home and commercial fishtanks. Sell to pet shops and aquarium dealers. Advertise in fish-related trade journals.

Artificial Plants. Make your specialty artificial flowers and plants. Sell a selection of arrangements, baskets, and special occasion creations; take custom orders.

Baby Clothes. Specialize in bargain-priced new and hand-me-down infant clothing and supplies. Offer an alteration service; take in trades to refurbish and resell.

Before you buy something, ask yourself, "Where am I going to put it?" and make sure that you have a clearly defined place in mind.

Tackle big tasks a bit at a time. Straightening every closet in the house might take days; one closet, especially one that hasn't gotten too cluttered, may take no longer than 15 or 20 minutes.

Baby-Sitting. Go to clients' homes by appointment and stay with the children for an hourly fee. Charge extra for two or more children, doing housework, or taking the kids out.

Baby Pictures. With still or video camera, arrange with hospital staff to photograph newborns (with parents, nurses, visitors). Sell print sets to proud parents.

Baby-Sitting Service. Accumulate a list of qualified, bonded sitters. Advertise your service and rates, deliver and pick up sitters. Collect fees and pay sitters a percentage.

Banquet Decorating. Take full charge of banquet room preparation: theme decorations, seating arrangements, centerpieces, etc. Advertise your service and list with the Chamber of Commerce.

Beauty Aids. Sell general or specialized beauty supplies in your home salon or by appointment. Represent established lines and/or sell your own brand.

Beauty Service. Set up a salon in your spare room with an outside entrance. Offer regular or specialized beauty care and treatments, permanents, etc. by appointment.

Bonsai Plants. Grow (or buy) and arrange in attractive pots or arrangements. Retail from your home, through ads, or wholesale to flower shops, greenhouses, and nurseries.

Book Reviewing. If qualified, read current books for publishers or agents. Write reviews to be quoted in book promotions or media reviews; work toward writing your own column!

Bookkeeping Service. Provide a bookkeeping service to small businesses in your area. Expand to more complex systems and computers.

Calligraphy. Easily learned by an artistic person. Acquire work through ads and stationery stores. Print fancy menus, show cards, placecards, invitations, announcements, etc.

Candle Making. Turn a hobby into a profitable business. Design your own line, offer custom styling, scents, and special touches. Between custom orders, make standard items.

Carpet Cleaning. With steam shampoo equipment, clean and renew residential and commercial carpets. Contact rental agencies, apartments, and condos for wholesale jobs.

Simplify your life. Get rid of the clutter and the nonproductive activities.

Resolve to make every day count. Treat each day as a treasure. Self-talk yourself into accomplishing something new each day. Live for today, not always anticipating tomorrow.

Ceramics. Make ceramic pieces to retail, wholesale, and display in your "store." Sell greenware, kits, and supplies. Charge for finishing and firing pieces.

Child Pick-up Service. Pick up and deliver clients' kids to after-school sports, theater, and games. Pick up children and deliver to parties. Charge extra to stay with them until mom returns. (You will be required to obtain extra insurance for this business.)

Children's Town History. Write and illustrate a booklet about your town just for kids. Sell copies to doctors, dentists, stores, hospitals, and nursery schools.

Children's Room Decorator. Specialize in decorating nurseries and children's rooms. Offer varied "package" motifs. Work with or through suppliers for a commission.

Children's Clothing. Specialize in new (stylish and/or closeout) and outgrown children's clothes and accessories. Alter hand-me-downs, "pre-wash" jeans, monogram sweats.

China and Glass Dealer. Collect and deal in antiques and interesting china and glass items. Buy at auctions, private and public sales, and through your advertisements.

Client Listings. Contract to keep customer (or business) information lists: customer birthdays, purchases, credit records, price records, employee records.

Community Cookbook. Publish a theme- or organizational-oriented recipe collection with entries from each family member or department. Print and distribute for a fee.

Companion Service. Accompany lonely, ailing, or elderly people who are alone temporarily on shopping trips, to and from the doctor, on short tours, or when travelling longer distances.

Cooking Lessons. Give gourmet/ethnic/regional cooking, canning, and baking lessons in your specialty. Hold classes in your kitchen or by appointment in your students' kitchens.

Custom Cookbooks. Organize, decorate (personalize the cover), and custom print (on computer) client recipe collections into their own "family heirloom" cookbooks.

Custom Handicrafts. Use your talents to embroider, tat, sew, or crochet products for customers with

Refuse to be bored. Get out of the rut you are living in. Buy some flowers, search out a new client, cook a new dish, replace the familiar with the unfamiliar. Take time to smell a new rose.

limited time or talent. Make extra goods between custom orders.

Custom Clothing Designs. Paint, block print, or transfer unique or custom designs on smocks or aprons, or on fabrics to be used for clothing, curtains, or even upholstery.

Custom Knitting. Take orders for hand-knitted sweaters, stockings, and sets. Make popular sellers between orders; attach your label to all products!

Custom Tailoring. Offer the luxury of handmade clothing: shirts, skirts, coats, uniforms, suits. A good service to add to an alteration business when you feel competent enough to start from scratch.

Cut Flower Business. Grow and supply fresh-cut flowers to markets and florists in your area. Offer a variety of seasonal flowers or specialize in several greenhouse-grown varieties.

Directory Publishing. Publish local information booklets or maps: where to shop, eat, fish, or visit. Booklets can be given away or sold by paid advertisers and businesses.

T̲ake advantage of your moods. If there are tasks you don't feel like doing today, find those tasks you do feel like doing.

Doll Clothes. Difficult work for an expert seamstress, but pays well. Work with doll makers and collectors, sell at fairs and through advertisements in doll-related publications.

Doll Making. Use ceramic molds, hand paint and finish fine dolls to sell to collectors, children, and stores. Advertise in doll publications; attend doll shows.

Doll Collecting. Buy, sell, and trade fine and antique dolls with other collectors and make investments. Visit shows and fairs regularly to keep abreast of trends and prices.

It takes 21 consecutive days doing a new task before it becomes a habit. Don't give up on day 15.

Errand Service. Perform errands for individuals and businesses. Go to the corner store or across the country. Deliver or pick up messages, packages, and important papers.

Exercise for Seniors. Conduct daily low-impact aerobics classes and sessions for different categories (according to agility) of senior citizens at your place, or have stops on a daily route.

Exercise Companion. Serve as a walking or jogging companion for company, moral support, and extra protection (good in cities). Carry any necessary (legal) protection.

Flower Arranging. Arrange flowers for parties, banquets, and office functions, from general decor to head table centerpieces. Make up displays to sell through stores.

Flower Drying. Raise or buy dryable flowers and shrubs for retail and wholesale customers. Offer one-kind packets or custom arrangements; sell kits with complete instructions.

Garage Cleaning. Contract to clean out garages, sheds, and attics for individuals, rental agents, and absentee landlords. Get paid for the work *and* see if you can keep anything of value.

Garage Sale Service. Set up, promote, and manage garage sales for inexperienced or reluctant clients. Inventory, help price, and sell for a percentage of the proceeds.

Genealogy. Trace and document family archives. Provide records and related artifacts to descendants. Charge by the amount of research involved and the number of documents produced.

When you have to decide if you're going to discard something (or give it away), ask yourself, "Do I need the item or want the item?" If you answer "want," that usually means you might very well get rid of the item.

Ghostwriter. Write articles, letters, reports, speeches, and other papers for busy executives and those with little talent in this area. Provide signed agreements to clients.

Hobby Newsletter. Create a newsletter or directory for and about hobbyists and their crafts. Build readership by fostering participation, exchanging ideas, listing fairs and supply sources.

Hobby Kits. Sell do-it-yourself hobby kits in your field of expertise. Include step-by-step guidance and pictures to help beginners learn the craft.

Holiday, Special Events Baskets. Prepare holiday and special event baskets of fruit, flowers, and "goodies." Wholesale or consign to gift stores and advertise custom retail work.

Home Permanents. Specialize in giving home perms at clients' places. Go to offices, homes, hospitals, and senior citizen centers by appointment or on a route.

Homemaker's Helper. Provide temporary relief or assistance for sick, vacationing, or just plain "pooped"

Once you've organized your space, you have to keep it organized by maintaining the space on a regular basis. You will find the maintenance part of organization is the most important aspect. To help keep clutter under control, set aside one bowl or basket in a central location to temporarily house small objects that have no current home.

moms. Charge by the hour or by the job (more than a full-time helper).

Hospital Grooming. Assist patients with nail, hair, and skin care in hospitals and nursing homes. A license may not be needed to provide an appreciated service on a route.

Housecleaning. Offer one-time or periodic housecleaning service. Perform the heavy tasks (shampoo rugs, clean stoves, wash windows, wax floors, defrost refrigerator, etc.).

Instructional Videos, Cassettes. Make recordings of yourself or others teaching and demonstrating their crafts and specialties. Market via mail or wholesale to stores.

Invisible Mending/Weaving. Repair snags, tears, and burns in fine clothing and fabrics. Advertise locally, work with cleaners and clothing stores in your area.

Jewelry Sales. Sell inexpensive to fine jewelry to friends, through party plans, direct from advertisements, or wholesale to local stores. Compare suppliers constantly!

Jewelry Boxes. Make fine jewelry boxes (lined, lacquered, inlaid, shell-covered) for gift stores, catalog

Use a kitchen cutlery tray to store art supplies, children's crayons, pencils, etc.

sales, and retail sales. Add music works for extra profits.

Jewelry Creations. Use your talent and ingenuity to mass produce or individually create exquisite jewelry—anything from diamonds to sliced bamboo.

Jewelry Buying (Old). Buy old, worn out, or outdated jewelry for salvage. Rejuvenated antique jewelry is quite valuable! Sell "waste" only as salvage.

Kid Photo Dolls. Take or use photos of kids to make various size (up to full-size) paper dolls of clients' children. Cut out, seal in plastic, and mount in slot on sturdy plywood and base.

Live-in Agency. Check out both prospective employers and workers. Charge fee to find a reliable person to stay with an elderly person who would otherwise have to go to a nursing home.

Local Who's Who. Compile and publish a directory or index with biographical sketches of prominent people, heroes, and leaders of your area, past and present

Local Heroes. Research and write items about local heroes, scouts,

Use colored plastic rings to color code your keys. It makes it much easier to locate keys. Store in one central location so everyone in the family knows where all the keys are stored.

pioneers, or ancestors. Sell to local publications and again later as a complete collection.

Manicure Service. Provide nail care service in or from your "salon." Check needs in hospitals, nursing homes, even offices for workers on break.

Go through your house periodically, eliminating items you no longer want. One possible criterion: when you no longer notice a decorative object (such as a picture), it may be time to get rid of it.

Narrating. Use your speaking ability to narrate private or commercial movies, videos, demos, and advertisements. Sell taped versions for slide show presentations.

Native Plants. Become an expert on plants native to your locale. Grow, propagate, and improve species. Raise the value of your plants and seeds by enclosing an informative brochure in each pack.

Neckties. Make and sell exclusive handmade ties using exotic materials from all over the world. Offer a wide selection of designs, attach your exclusive label.

Needlecraft. Make homemade items to sell on consignment, to mail order catalog companies, or through parties and ads.

Party Packages. Make up and market complete party packages with innovative games, masks, favors, stunts, and entertainment for various age, size, and interest groups.

Party Planning. Take complete charge of a customer's planned party. Decorate, schedule activities, and send invitations. Arrange entertainment, catering, and cleanup.

Personalized Office Items. Make and/or sell personalized (engraved or monogrammed) office accessories: logos, coffee cups, desk signs, paperweights, briefcases, etc.

Pet Sitting. Feed, water, clean up after, and check on pets twice a day in their homes while owners are away. Call owners or the veterinarian if there are any problems.

Pet Hotel. Board and care for pets in your kennels or cages while owners are away. Or work with assistants who provide "foster homes" for unusual or pampered pets.

Pillows. Make and decorate designer, fancy, or country-style pillows to sell in and at boutiques, fairs, party plans, sales catalogs, and/or through advertisements and mail order.

Pomanders. Revive this wonderfully fragrant Egyptian art. Process oranges into hardened and long-lasting sachets. Use spices, perfume mixtures, and penetrating cloves, then sell!

Practice a 45/15 rule that really helps your workday. It works like this. After every 45-minute work cycle, take a 15-minute break and do something different—take a short walk, go outside for some fresh air, call someone on the phone, get a drink of water. This rule will keep you renewed and refreshed.

In planning the week's chores, try to set aside a free day (or at least a few hours) for yourself to do whatever you want—whether it's a day out of the house or time alone to finish that book you started several months ago.

Potted Plants. Plant and groom popular potted plants. Display in attractive settings, especially when they are in bloom or full foliage.

Pottery. With your potter's wheel, make, fire, and sell your own style of pottery. Teach techniques to students and put your "mark" on every piece you offer for sale.

Puppet Making. Create your own puppets (carton caricatures or custom faces). Give shows at children's parties, train both "actors" and puppet makers. Sell kits.

Quilting. Make and sell beautiful homemade quilts from "scraps" in your spare time. Take color photographs of each quilt and make a catalog to show customers your work.

Rag Dolls. Make and sell rag, sock, and other stuffed dolls in your own unique fashion. Attach your label and offer to stores in your area and via mail nationwide.

Reading to Patients. Visit hospitals, nursing homes, or individual homes and read stories and novels to patients. If time is limited, read a chapter a week. Charge relatives.

Recipe Sales. Perfect your favorite recipes. Promote and sell them individually, in small sets, or as part of collections. Sell something that will make the cook look great!

Report Writing. Write information or "how-to" articles on subjects in which you are well versed. Sell to technical publications or advertise and sell reports direct.

Résumé Service. Launch a professional résumé-writing service. Interview clients and review their qualifications. Customize resumes for types of jobs sought.

Rug Making. Make and sell hand-woven rugs in standard and custom designs. Offer instructions, materials, and do-it-yourself kits, plus related supplies and equipment.

Scarecrows. Make and sell authentic scarecrows for gardeners and garden displays. Also, sell kits, complete with frames, straw, and old clothes and face parts.

Seed Packets. Collect, sort, label, and sell packets of selected wildflowers or plants native to your area. Include instructions, history, and folklore on each package.

Learn how to cut off time-consuming calls without hurting people's feelings. For example, it's quite all right to say, "This is a terrible time for me, may I call you back?" (Of course, do call back later.)

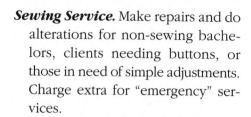

Try to get the first appointment of the morning so that you won't be delayed by someone ahead of you and you'll still have most of the day left when you finish.

Sewing Service. Make repairs and do alterations for non-sewing bachelors, clients needing buttons, or those in need of simple adjustments. Charge extra for "emergency" services.

Sewing Classes. If qualified, hold sewing classes in your home. Offer full courses as well as special "how-to" seminars for specific techniques. Sell material and supplies to students.

Shopping Service. Do grocery shopping for clients. Get their list, then buy and deliver groceries. Use your shopping skills, pricing experience, and volume buying to get the best values.

Shut-in Service. Call and/or visit temporary or permanent shut-ins on behalf of absentee relatives. Take them magazines, play games with them, read to them, and be their friend.

Soapmaking. Learn as a hobby or adjunct to candlemaking. Create and sell various shapes, colors, and fragrances. Mold prepared solutions or make your soap from scratch.

Stenciling Art. Design your own stencils for interesting fabric designs.

Apply to clothing and fabrics to sell. Sell stencils, fabric kits, pats, dyes, and supplies.

Storytelling. Narrate stories at children's parties. Use props (dolls, pets, puppets) and audience participation. Perfect the stories, then tape or put down on paper.

Tailoring. Use your skills to custom-tailor men's, women's, or children's garments (including jackets, uniforms, and suits) in or from your home "shop." Attach your own label.

Telephone Canvassing. Contract with salesmen or businesses to obtain leads or potential customer information for them from your telephone operation. Charge by the lead.

Terrariums. Start and nurture plants in bottles and plastic containers that require little (if any) watering. Grow plants to peak of attractiveness and sell, container and all.

Town History. If none exists, publish a booklet about your town. Sell direct and/or to merchants for resale or to give away. (Consider including paid advertisements.)

Give yourself deadlines. Color-code the due date on your calendar so you can visually see that date each day. You might even color-code a few immediate dates along the way to make sure you are on track. Write it down.

Tutoring. Provide assistance by appointment or scheduled classes to students or anyone in need of your expertise, whether the subject is academic, technical, or operational.

Typing Service. Do typing jobs in your home for doctors, lawyers, businesspeople, and students.

Used Book Sales. Buy, sell, and trade used books, novels, reference, science, text, even collector editions, from your home.

Vitamin Sales. Sell one or more lines of vitamins and supplements, some with generic or your name "brand." Advertise and/or enlist users/helpers and party plans.

Wedding Consultant. Plan and coordinate weddings from start to finish: decor, guest lists, dresses, schedules, catering, photographer, etc. Receive fee and commissions.

Word Processing. Produce "editable" drafts and finished professional letters, manuscripts, and documents for students, lawyers, writers, and businesses. Allow editing prior to final printing.

These are only suggestions to get your creative juices flowing. Think of what you know how to do, what you like to do, and what could make you some extra money. Then start doing it!

Appendix

The Home-Based Business Plan

A business plan is one of the essential ingredients to a successful business. However, because the home-based business is unique, it calls for its own type of business plan. Here are some very simple guidelines for completing a realistic plan for your own business. Refer back to chapter 4 (Business Goals) for a more in-depth description of each component.

I. Determine the plan

A. *Prayerfully choose your family ideal or mission statement. Write it below.*

_____

_____

_____

B. *Determine family priorities and goals.*

Priority #1:

_____

_____

_____

Priority #2:

_____

_____

_____

Priority #3:

_____

_____

_____

Priority #4:

_____

_____

_____

Priority #5:

_____

_____

_____

C. *Determine business goals.*

1. Business Goal #1:

_____

_____

_____

Estimated date of completion:

_____

2. Business Goal #2:

_____

_____

_____

Estimated date of completion:

_____

3. Business Goal #3:

_____

_____

_____

Estimated date of completion:

_____

4. Business Goal #4:

_____

_____

_____

Estimated date of completion:

_____

5. **Business Goal #5:**

_____

_____

_____

Estimated date of completion:

_____

D. *Determine long-term goals.*

6 month goals:

1) _____

2) _____

3) _____

4) _____

How will I achieve each of these goals?

_____

_____

_____

1 year goals:

1) _____

2) _____

3) _____

4) _____

How will I achieve each of these goals?

_____

_____

_____

II. Total mess to total rest
How do I intend to organize my office and keep it that way?

A. *Organizational method:*

_____

B. *Maintenance method:*

_____

III. Obtaining needed resources

A. *Equipment*

1. Immediate needs:

_____

_____

_____

2. Needs within the first 6 months:

_____

_____

_____

3. Needs within the first year:

_____

_____

_____

4. Projection for needs within 5 years:

_____

_____

_____

B. *Furniture*

1. Immediate needs:

_____

_____

_____

2. Needs within the first 6 months:

_____

_____

_____

3. Needs within the first year:

_____

_____

_____

4. Projection for needs within 5 years:

_____

_____

_____

C. *Supplies*

1. Immediate needs:

_____

_____

_____

2. Needs within the first 6 months:

_____

_____

_____

3. Needs within the first year:

_____

_____

_____

4. Projection for needs within 5 years:

_____

_____

_____

IV. Marketing your business

A. *Finding your customer. List up to 10 advertising/marketing ideas you plan to utilize in marketing your business:*

1. _____

    Estimated expense: $_____

2. _____

    Estimated expense: $_____

3. _____

    Estimated expense: $_____

4. _____

    Estimated expense: $_____

5. _____

    Estimated expense: $_____

6. _____

    Estimated expense: $_____

7. _____

    Estimated expense: $_____

8. _____

    Estimated expense: $_____

9. _____

    Estimated expense: $_____

10. _____

    Estimated expense: $_____

B. *Product/service pricing*

V. Maintain the balance between the family and the business

A. *Set working schedule.*

What hours will you work each day?

_____

B. *Set aside time for your husband.*

Will you set aside a particular day or evening each week for your spouse? If so, what day?

_____

_____

C. *Set aside time for the children.*

What activities will you schedule with your children on a daily/weekly basis?

_____

_____

_____

VI. Visualize your financial goals and see them realized

A. *Set realistic and obtainable goals.*

1. Monthly financial goal:

   _____

   What will this money be used for?

   _____

   _____

   _____

   How will we achieve the monthly financial goals?

   _____

   _____

   _____

2. What will we do with any "extra" money?

   _____

   _____

   _____

3. What will we do if we do not meet our monthly financial goal?

   _____

   _____

   _____

B. *Set a goal of being in the "black" the first year.*

Ideas for reaching this goal:

_____

_____

_____

VII. Reevaluate consistently

Evaluate your stated priorities and goals often and make updates and changes when necessary.

_____

_____

_____

_____

_____

_____

_____

Notes

1. Paul and Sarah Edwards, *Working from Home: Everything You Need to Know About Living and Working Under the Same Roof* (New York: G.P. Putnam's Sons, 1994), pp. 297-99.

2. "The Parent Trap," *Newsweek* magazine, September 7, 1998, pp. 52-59.

3. Larry Burkett, *Women Leaving the Workplace* (Chicago: Moody Press, 1995), p. 99.

4. Deborah Shouse, "Mom's the One," from *Family Circle,* quoted in *Reader's Digest,* August 1997, p. 110.

5. Burkett, *Women Leaving,* p. 86.

6. Ibid., p. 247.

7. Ibid., pp. 250-51.

8. Personal interview, Computer Options store, San Bernardino, CA.

9. Edwards, *Working from Home,* p. 488.

10. Ibid., p. 489.

11. Ibid., p. 499.

12. Personal interview with Shirley Taylor, Taylor Business Group, Lake Forest, CA.

13. Edwards, *Working from Home,* pp. 269-76.